ADVANCE PRAISE

"If there's one person in the world that can help motivate you to take action, it's Scott. His years of experience, combined with his care to actually help people live a better life, are put into The Take Action Effect. You'd be doing yourself and the important people around you a disservice not to read this book and start changing your life."

—PAT FLYNN, FOUNDER OF SMART PASSIVE INCOME

"Scott is truly an entrepreneur on fire, and has proven that taking action leads to results. In this book you'll learn through his life and business experiences how to shortcut your path to building a true lifestyle business. This book is seriously ON FIRE with value bombs and a clear roadmap so you can take action...and IGNITE!"

—JOHN LEE DUMAS, FOUNDER AND HOST OF THE *ENTREPRENEURS ON FIRE!* PODCAST

"*Scott is a shining example of how taking action can revolutionize your life. He's not only built an amazing life for himself using these tactics, he's helped so many people achieve the life of their dreams. Your first action is to read and use the content in this book NOW! It can change the trajectory of your life.*"

—JAIME MASTERS, HOST OF *EVENTUAL MILLIONAIRE* PODCAST, OWNER OF EVENTUALMILLIONAIRE. COM AND OWNERBOX.COM

"*I've known Scott (aka: Scotty V) for a few years now and his TAKE ACTION approach that he shares is exactly what people need to get out of their own way and be successful. Inside The Take Action Effect, Scott shows you how to discover your hidden talent and then build a business around it, while not chasing the next shiny object. This book is the roadmap to follow for anyone wanting to build a real business that they love.*"

—RYAN LEE, SERIAL ENTREPRENEUR AND BUILDER OF MULTIPLE BUSINESSES, RYANLEE.COM

"*Scott has taken a lifetime of reinventing success time and time again and shares the secrets to this path to financial freedom in simple-to-understand steps. This book is a game changer for anyone who wants to level up their business.*"

—AZUL TERRONEZ, CEO OF AUTHORS WHO LEAD

"*Just five minutes with Scott could be worth thousands of dollars for your business. This book gives you way more than that and could be exactly what gets your business to the next level. The best action you can take right now is to buy this book.*"

—BRYAN COHEN, *USA TODAY* BESTSELLING AUTHOR AND CEO OF BEST PAGE FORWARD

"*If anyone knows the inner workings of what it takes to build a business that can stand the test of time, it's Scott. This book will give you the roadmap you need to get out there and make your dreams a reality.*"

—DAVID YOUNG, FOUNDER OF DRONE LAUNCH ACADEMY

"*It's rare to find an industry leader with Scott's vision and know-how. Unlike many, he shares strategies to create and grow a business that's built to last, far surpassing those teachings of the gold rush mentality.*"

—ALEXANDRA JIMENEZ, FOUNDER OF TRAVEL FASHION GIRL

"*This is a powerful resource for any entrepreneur! Whether you're just getting started or have been in the business world for years, Scott has created an insightful book which can help any marketer get unstuck, uncover your hidden superpowers, and create your roadmap for success. Take action and grab your copy if you want to create a future-proof business!*"

—MONICA LOUIE, FACEBOOK AND INSTAGRAM ADS STRATEGIST AT MONICALOUIE.COM

"*Scott is one of the few people you meet who always exceeds expectations. He has an amazing ability to break even the most complex topics into easy-to-understand, digestible chunks, and this book falls perfectly in line with that theme. The Take Action Effect is the perfect roadmap for how to use the smallest moments in your life to grab the reins of your own future, get out of your own way, and start TAKING ACTION.*"

"*The more I get to know Scott, the more I realize we are two peas in a pod: same humble backgrounds, the same belief system of how to treat people, and never putting money over people. Where Scott excels though, is his undeniable energy and ability to motivate people. If you read this book, follow Scott's teachings, and TAKE ACTION, success will seemingly come naturally.*"

"*Scott is a perfect example of how to take an idea and turn it into reality. This book shares the exact roadmap he's used to uncover your personal strengths and create an ACTION plan that will lead to freedom. The wisdom he shares in this book is pure gold and could change your life.*"

"*Every time I have a conversation with Scott, I walk away feeling clear, focused, and motivated to make big things happen! If you've ever struggled to get things to 'click' in your business, this book is a must-read!*"

—JILL STANTON, SCREWTHENINETOFIVE.COM

"*Scott has helped me see the power of taking action, which has led to me achieving massive growth in my business, including leaving my job to work on my business full-time. In this book, Scott walks through how to take the right actions to achieve your goals.*"

—KEVIN SANDERSON, FOUNDER OF
MAXIMIZING ECOMMERCE

"*Scott is the man! The main reason people don't progress with their business is because they don't take action. But with this book, you'll be inspired to get up off your butt and build a lasting business you can be proud of. Highly recommended!*"

—STEVE CHOU, FOUNDER OF MY WIFE QUIT HER JOB

"*Scotty V. is a leading voice in the ecommerce world, specializing in brand building. However, it is his unwavering commitment to helping his seller community succeed that has led to the profitability of so many. It's definitely time to bring his voice to print! I'm excited to finally have a book filled with his clear and actionable strategies that I can recommend to any and all sellers.*"

—GREG MERCER, CEO AND FOUNDER OF JUNGLE SCOUT

THE TAKE ACTION EFFECT

THE
TAKE
ACTION
EFFECT

**PROVEN STEPS TO BUILD A FUTURE-PROOF BUSINESS
AND CREATE YOUR ULTIMATE FREEDOM**

SCOTT VOELKER

LIONCREST

PUBLISHING

THE TAKE ACTION EFFECT

Proven Steps to Build a Future-Proof Business
& Create Your Ultimate Freedom

ISBN   978-1-5445-0281-6 *Hardcover*

978-1-5445-0280-9 *Paperback*

978-1-5445-0279-3 *Ebook*

To my wife, Lisa, who has always been there, supporting me
and believing in me, even when I didn't. You are my ROCK!

My kids, Alexis, Scotty, and Kayla, for giving me purpose
and showing me what it feels like to truly love.

My father, who taught me how to be honest, to be
loyal, and to work hard at every part of my life.

My mother, who's no longer with us but taught me how
to be open and playful even when times are tough.

CONTENTS

INTRODUCTION

—

Treat this like it's yours. One day it will be.

That was the quiet promise my dad offered when I worked for him at the construction company he owned with a past coworker and friend. Before that, I never would have thought it would be possible for me, a kid who barely graduated high school, to own my own business. You have to know that about me to understand how great it felt to work hard every day knowing that there was a possibility that one day this business could be mine. Even though I was working hard every day, I really enjoyed the work we were doing for our customers.

Every morning I would show up to the office and sit down with my construction crews to plan out the day's work. I loved those mornings—coffee in hand, of course—and the long days were worth every second. I could go to bed at night knowing that I was another day closer to having and owning my own business that would support my young family.

The feeling was way different than what I'd gotten from the work I'd done in the past. Right out of high school, I spent some time working for a cable company first and then for Quad Graphics—a major printing company that published some big magazines. I did that for about nine months, and I thought it was my ticket to success. The printing company was a good enough job that I thought would turn into a long-term career, but I quickly discovered I absolutely *hated* it. I couldn't spend my whole life feeling trapped inside a factory for twelve hours a day. That type of career was definitely not for me. I had to make a change, but what else could I do? Fortunately, an unexpected chain of events opened new doors.

This moment, when I realized I didn't want to be stuck inside at the printing company, is what I now call a "Take Action Moment." These are moments in life—moments that you have probably already experienced—when we make a decision to take some kind of action, and they often open new doors and opportunities without us even realizing it. Throughout this book, not only are we going to learn to recognize the Take Action Moments in our past, but we'll learn how to make them happen on purpose as we create the life we want.

I'll explain a bit more. See, my dad also had a planned career laid out in front of him. He'd worked at General Electric for years and thought for sure it would be his career for the rest of his life. The corporation had other ideas, though. When he and a good friend of his were laid off at the same time, they joined up and started doing odd jobs to cover the bills. Soon, it grew into something of a construction business—two guys, a pickup truck, and a need for some extra help. When my dad offered me a job for seven bucks an hour (and plenty of time *not* being stuck inside a building!), I took it without telling him that I didn't even know how to read a tape measure. Heck, I'd never built anything in my life at this point, except maybe a tree fort in the woods with my buddies. This opportunity was too good to pass up, and I was pretty excited!

I hustled past the awkward learning stages, scrambling to learn the correct measurements on a job site, and my dad mentored me in the trade. The company continued to grow, and so did I, until we had sixteen employees and I oversaw all of the crews. Now it was my job to lead all of the workers at each site to get the job done right and on time.

It felt like the impossible was right in front of me: I was

going to be a business owner one day. Right then, all I could see was the path laid out ahead of me. Through a lot of hard work and some patience from my father, I'd learned a trade, earned some flexibility, and had the chance to become a business owner. Over and over, I was told the business would become mine. It was within my reach. All I had to do was stick with it.

Of course, this book wouldn't have happened if I'd stayed there. The future's never exactly what we plan it out to be, is it?

I had a regular schedule each day, generally starting with a stop at a local coffee shop: I would drive to the office, get the guys off to their jobs, and check in with them throughout the day. I worked hard wherever I was needed, and stayed late to get the job done after everyone else left at four or five. My dad saw my work ethic and had always trusted me because of it. He gave me plenty of freedom to do things however I needed to, as long as the job got done. His partner trusted me, too. At least, I thought he did.

The questions started coming slowly at first—*Where are you? What are you doing right now?* Then with more accusations from him—*I feel like you're wasting time. What are those coffee stops in the morning all about, after all?* The last straw was when he brought my dad in on it. Turns out, that's what it was all about—the business partner had been spying on me and then reporting the time back to my father. What he said next...well, it blew me away. "If you add all that time up," he'd reported angrily, "we're paying Scott for *an hour* a week *to drink coffee!*"

...You've got to be kidding me.

I stormed into the office as soon as I realized what was happening.

"Let me get this straight. I'm busting my ass to make sure your jobs get done on time so that you can pay your employees and keep your business *barely* above water... but a ten-minute stop for coffee is the deal breaker? Are you serious right now?"

This was the line in the sand, no question.

"If that's the way you want this to go," I told him, "then I'll be sure to leave at five o'clock on the dot every day. If I don't stay late, the jobs don't get done. *Good luck* running payroll checks when they come due and stuff's not done."

My bright future was dulled. I felt pissed. I felt tired.

And I felt completely stuck.

FAST FORWARD TO TODAY

I've always loved the freedom to choose how I started my morning so much there's no way I could have imagined how great it could be. Not only do I have morning coffee with my wife by the pool almost every day, but lunch, too—not to mention the flexibility to coach my kids, attend every school event, and pick them up and drop them off every day. There's absolutely no way I could have imagined seven dollars an hour turning into seven figures a year and a lifestyle of freedom.

I'm not feeling stuck anymore, but every day I work with people who are. It took me a long time to get out of that rut. It took a long time to get from being spied on every day to hosting a podcast with more than 13 million downloads and a daily schedule that's entirely my own. People reach out to me with questions, and I hear from listeners literally all over the world. Others come to me for high-level personal coaching in my Inner Circle, where we brainstorm through their businesses to increase revenue and scale.

I suppose you want to hear about the income shift—from seven bucks to seven figures—but that's not even important to me anymore. I'd rather make less and be with my family, enjoying the hours this life is giving us, versus being able to say I made a certain amount.

It's not about the money. It's about the impact on my

family and on the people I help achieve their own freedom on a regular basis. Ironically, when you reach that point in your life and in your business-building, the money almost always follows. At least it has for me, over and over again.

HOW DID THIS HAPPEN IN THE FIRST PLACE?

There are so many ways to get yourself stuck. For me, I felt like my options were limited. I didn't have a college degree to fall back on—heck, I didn't even spend a day in college—or the experience that I thought I'd need to set off on my own. When you think your career or business is *the one*, you invest so much into it that it's hard to imagine doing anything else.

Have you ever felt like that? So many people do. It's totally normal. You put so much work in to get where you are. Maybe you have a specialized degree or a trade certification that took years to obtain. You might still be paying on the loans it took to get there. Or you've spent years building up experience, like I did in construction, without anything else to fall back on. You might have even built a business yourself—reaching out and taking the freedom that we all want, only to find that it's turned into a J-O-B again and you're just as exhausted and burned out as ever.

For a while, more money seems like the answer. If you just had more money, you'd be able to breathe a little bit.

Maybe you wouldn't have to work as much in that job or business that's draining the life out of you.

It didn't take me very long to realize that money wasn't what I was after, though, and you might already be there. No matter what you're looking for—whether it's money or freedom or anything else—getting there can feel impossible. You obviously can't repeat the steps that you followed to get to where you are. That'd take another degree or another decade of experience or another big investment of time and money. This time, you're not a kid just starting out in life, either. This time, you've got a family to support.

When I realized I didn't actually want to stick around until the construction company was mine, I felt like I was looking out of a narrow scope as I looked for possibilities. The only thing I knew I could do was to work for someone and get paid. I never once thought that I could leverage experience or the strength of others to build a company.

After spending a lot of time in one place, we feel like we have to stay there. It took all that time to get there, so how can we possibly start over? How do we replace that income, this time doing what we want to do? Those questions keep us stuck, but I want to pose them as a challenge to you. What do you *want* to do? I know it's possible for you to do it, and I'm going to show you how.

The fun part is exploring all the ways you can put it into action.

I HAVE FAITH IN YOU—DO *YOU*?

I'm not going to lie. This is an important moment. You're holding *The Take Action Effect* because you know it's time to do something. I wrote this book because I believe you can do something—something *big*.

The big thing that you accomplish will look different than mine, but underneath it's all the same. You want to make a living without sacrificing your freedom or getting knocked down by an unpredictable future. That's it.

If you're still thinking, "Sure, plenty of people could make that work, but that doesn't mean I can," let's break this down. Maybe you've got a college degree. How did you get your degree? I'm sure there were times you didn't want to study. There were times you didn't want to drag yourself to class. But you did. You made it. Maybe you've created a business. Were there some struggles to get past? What about the first days on your job, without any experience at all, degree or no? How about that career you built as you climbed the corporate ladder and did what it took to succeed—was every meeting, every confrontation a walk in the park? You've done big things already. This is just a different kind of big.

To really pull this off, you'll first have to get clear about what drives you.

For a long time, I kept thinking that what I wanted was the money. When I worked at the printing company, straight out of high school, I knew I could work up in the ranks. Back then, a first pressman was making $70,000–$80,000 a year, which is worth about double that in today's dollars. Even though I started out at the printing company as a jogger, just moving the pieces that were coming off of the machines that the pressmen were running, if I just kept working up the ranks for four or six years or so, there was a promise of a decent career.

We choose our careers based on how much money we can make and do all kinds of work to get there. Once you make it, good luck if you don't like it. You're more or less screwed. I know people who have spent four to six years and $300,000 or more on their education, only to find out that it wasn't what they really wanted to do. The sunk cost is only part of it, too. More than anything, pressure from our families and ourselves can keep us stuck on paths we don't love.

If you do get to make money on that path, you quickly learn that making money takes time. Time on call, time away from families, time building and chasing and working. At some point, you're not even enjoying the few hours that you do get with your family. We get excited when we finally earn three whole weeks of vacation out of an entire year spent burned out and exhausted.

That's totally crazy—yet we accept it as normal.

If you're enjoying your sixty-plus-hour weeks because you love what you're doing that much, then by all means, keep it up. I'd say that's not the case for most of us. Even when we've got the house, we've got the cars, and the kids are taken care of, we're miserable. Is that money worth it if it's taking away from our relationships, our kids, and ourselves?

It's not just about the money, is it?

The promise of money wasn't enough to keep me at the printing company. Deep down, I needed fresh air. I needed to move. I needed space. So I followed a similar path at my dad's company. Start out at the bottom, work hard, make it to the top—this time, for the freedom instead of money. When I found out my freedom was limited there, too, I lost that fire again. I needed something more. I thought working from home would be the answer, and though I made that happen pretty quickly as we built up a photography business from scratch, it still wasn't enough. (More on the photography business later.) That kind of work still left me tied down to a schedule, which meant my dream opportunity had turned into another restrictive job.

So I'll ask you again: why are you *really* feeling stuck? Think about everything you've done to get this far in life. You've built up a career, trade, or business once already. Maybe you've done it more than once. It's not the work or your limitations that have you scared and wondering how you can get out of this mess.

It's not that you *can't* do the work. More likely, you think you'll have to do all that same work, just to end up stuck all over again. You need some help taking the right steps.

LET ME WALK WITH YOU

The grass isn't always greener. You might not want the responsibility of a business, and the last thing I want is to see you spend more time building toward another thing that isn't what you want out of life.

That's why, before we get into anything tactical or practical, we're going to spend time figuring out who you are and what you want out of life. You're going to have to shift your mindset before anything else.

Just in this introduction, I've asked you to look at your past accomplishments from a different perspective. That college degree, work experience, or corporate ladder climb may seem like the path that pigeonholed you into a job you're tired of now—but those experiences are also important clues about your drive and your desire. You've done a ton of work, and that means you are capable of even more.

Now I want you to turn that into fuel: you've sacrificed a lot of time and energy to get here. Why wouldn't you sacrifice just a little bit more to create a life that you love? The one you *want*? You've put in the time. You've friggin' earned it. Why would you let anything at all stop you? It's time to take action to make that life happen!

FORGET THE GET RICH QUICK

The steps I'll lay out for you will help you identify what you want out of life, what you want out of your business, and the exact process that bridges the two. Then you'll develop a plan to build a flexible, lasting business, or one that you sell so you can start something new. Those steps can be repeated over and over again to shape and reshape your brand and business in any space—from e-commerce to digital products and everything in between—because flexible businesses are future-proof businesses.

For now, though, don't worry about doing everything at

once. This doesn't have to be overwhelming. You just need to learn the process.

I'm not going to ask you to leave your job, quit your business, or focus 100 percent of your time to this. Remember, I've followed these steps and I've coached other people through them, and at no point did we drop everything and risk our families just to say we had gone "all in." That kind of ask usually comes with a get-rich-quick promise, and it leads to people quitting their jobs prematurely or bailing on the businesses that they've built, losing their money, and winding up more stressed than they started.

Worse than that, if you think you're supposed to get rich quick and then you don't, you may think you've failed— and you may give up. In a take action mindset, you haven't actually failed *until* you've given up. Problems and setbacks aren't failures; they're experience.

WHAT IS...*THE TAKE ACTION EFFECT?*

If failing is experience, winning is a result. Every action you take has an outcome, and whether the result is a win or a loss, it helps you learn. When you begin to take action toward your dream, you'll make some wrong moves, guaranteed. Maybe you didn't run the right ad, pick the right product, or nail the right messaging. Maybe you didn't pick the right career, take the right promotion, or build the right life. So what result did you get? Why did it work? Why didn't it work? What did you learn?

Before we can ask these questions—and get the answers that move us forward—we have to take action. When you try something new, however small, you get to see what happens, ask questions, and get a result. Those small victories are big wins, because they drive the engine behind the take action effect.

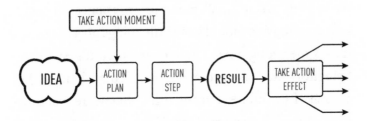

The "all in" that a take action mindset asks for is the kind that says you're not going to dabble. You're committing to this process—to following these steps. You're going to show up and do the work, even when it looks like nothing good has happened yet. There's so much power in that commitment that we're going to spend the first part of this book building a solid foundation with a take action mindset.

In part 2, we'll get into action steps as you start to future-proof your business and life. Those chapters are all about putting the process in place. First, you'll see how to design a side hustle that you dedicate a few hours to every day. If you already have a business online, you can take these steps we'll be covering and add them to help you grow and future-proof your current brand.

From there, I'll show you how to build that into the business that supports your ideal lifestyle until your ideal becomes your reality.

TIME TO TAKE ACTION

We're going to start small, focusing every ounce of energy into one step at a time. Those little things go a long way. It took me a long time to understand that. It's easy now to identify the "take action moments" that changed the course of my life. But at the time, they were just ordinary things. Going out with my friends, buying a different computer on a friend's recommendation, recording a podcast while I learned something new—none of those steps felt big, but they did require action. The effect? An incredible life that I barely let myself dream about before.

This book isn't the whole house. I don't know what kind of shingles you need on your roof. But I can offer you a blueprint. I can help you with the steps you need to take and the order you need to go in. I can make it clear and easy to follow so that you never sit down for an hour without knowing exactly what action you'll take to get closer to your goals.

Before, you were ambitious for yourself. Now you're fighting for yourself *and* your family. Before, you wanted a label. You wanted to show off your high school graduation, diploma, or promotions to your friends and family. *Look at my badge of honor! I did it!* Before, you didn't realize you'd wake up one day miserable and that badge wouldn't do anything for you anymore. But the discomfort you feel now—the discomfort of being stuck—comes from outgrowing who you were before. Growth asks us to strive toward the next thing.

Now you know more about who you are and what you enjoy. Now you have more experience, wisdom, education, and talents. Now you can figure out what the heck you actually want. And then? Go get it.

PART 1

CREATE A MINDSET OF ACTION

BREAKING THE CHAINS

———

Seven dollars an hour—I'll never forget that number. That's how much my dad offered me when he asked me to work at his construction company. Not only did it seem like a good income at the time, but it came with so much promise. I thought that if I could learn a trade, it would become something that no one could take away from me. I'd always have those skills, no matter what the future brought.

Man, at the time, the future seemed so clear.

I was exactly where I needed to be. Our family tradition had been to find something that would last and work hard at it. My father worked a trade, and his father had, too. Of my dad's nine siblings, some of them only went to school until the eighth grade so that they could help out on the family farm. College was never on the table—I had to find a trade.

From a young age, it was drilled into my head that when you find something and learn it, you'll have that thing until you die. Right out of high school, I went to work in places that might have a future. I worked at a cable company for a little bit and then a printing company where I thought I might stay long-term. While it did have promise, it also felt totally claustrophobic. There was something more I wanted out of my life, and my dad's offer seemed like the answer.

Construction offered two things: plenty of variety in going from job to job, with lots of time outdoors, filling in wherever I was needed—and the promise that I'd not only have a good income in the future but also a business that would one day be mine. So without knowing a thing about construction, I took the job right away.

Obviously, I'm not doing construction anymore. It didn't last into the future like I'd hoped it would, though I have used those skills since then and technically could still fall back on them if I needed to. I guess the promise held up, in theory.

Honestly, though, I'm not sorry that it didn't last.

Every twist and turn in my life has led to a new opportunity. If my dad hadn't lost his own trade when GE laid him off, he wouldn't have started that business. If that business hadn't grown stale for me (okay, if his business partner hadn't spied on me—reread the introduction if you missed that), I wouldn't have walked away and into something new. I wouldn't be writing this today.

But before I could work my way toward my own truly future-proof business and life, I had to face the facts: I'd gotten myself stuck, and it was going to take a lot of hard work to get out of it.

HOW'D THIS EVEN HAPPEN?

Because I was told the construction business would be my own one day, I leaned into the work and helped them build it up into something worth keeping. From the time I was nineteen years old, I did what I needed to do to build up the business. I'd work sixty-plus hours a week, no matter what. By the time I was twenty-one, I was married and had a baby. My wife would hate it when I'd wake up sick and still go to work, but there were goals ahead! After my sixty-plus-hour week, I was also slowly building my own house after hours and on the weekends. I was not afraid of hard work and putting in the time. Every morning, I'd get up early and do it all over again.

(Side note: When people say they don't have time to build

a business on the side, I tell them I built a *house* on the side. I might enjoy a lot of the fruits of a successful business now, but I know how much hard work it takes to get there. You can do it. I promise.)

About seven years in, I started to wear down. We were making more hires, some of which were family members of my father's business partner. That never works out well, and sure enough, we started to have some internal issues. My extra hours weren't building the business anymore, but instead they were keeping us above water. I wasn't even going in sick because I was looking forward to the future, I was going in because we were always a week away from not making payroll and I didn't want to let the company down. It wasn't being run well from the top, and the stress to get the jobs done fell on my shoulders. This business wasn't what I thought it was.

Then the whole spying incident happened, and *worn down* turned into *beaten down*. There had to be a better way, but how? I'd poured most of my twenties and all of my experience into this one company. I had no other qualifications and no idea where to go next. I was stuck with no way out.

TIME OUT

Listen, I don't want this book to be all about me. This is really about you and your story as it unfolds. So let's pause for a second and talk about you. What have you done in your life that you've worked hard for? You might not have even known whether it was going to work—but you still did it.

Maybe you put in the work for six or eight years to get a degree. Maybe you built a business. Maybe you climbed the ladder. The point is, you've definitely achieved things in your life already because you saw a prize at the end and decided to go after it. So what's your prize here? What's it going to take to reach it? Look to the past to remind yourself that you can do it, and look to your potential future to remind yourself why you should.

FROM HERE TO...WHERE?

We've all felt it. There are those moments of hope when it seems like the road ahead is clear, but then once you step back for a second you think, *Wait a minute—I want out, but this is all I know.* That moment hurts.

Being stuck doesn't look the same for everyone. I talked to one person not long ago who had built up six figures *a month* in revenue but felt like they didn't have any brand traction. They didn't know how to move away from the shotgun approach that got them to that point. Someone else in my Inner Circle private coaching group created an e-commerce business that exploded, and now he feels like he can't keep up. Meanwhile, too many people to count reach out to me trying to figure out how to get started with any kind of business at all, because the job they are in is sucking the life out of them.

The important thing here is not that you're stuck. You already knew that. What I want you to know is that you're not alone. I've been there as someone just starting out, and I've been there as someone whose business has turned into yet another job (we'll get to that part of the story soon).

Our circumstances might be different, but the way out is the same. It's not just taking action once but understanding the take action effect that makes the difference. It's about what happens after you make a decision, take an action, and experience a result.

Right now, that feeling of being stuck is a result. You've put time and effort and money into your life, and the result is not what you hoped it would be. What actions made it happen?

Maybe you've given a company everything you've got but they've decided to downsize and leave you out in the cold. Maybe you're feeling like the business you've built has started running *you*. Maybe you picked a degree or a trade path because of the career it promised but figured out too late that the job isn't a good fit.

It's not just that you're unhappy with where you are, is it? In my experience, it's more than that. Deep down, you know that where you are is a result of the actions you've taken. You feel like if you start over again, you'll just do those same familiar, comfortable actions all over again, and that means you'll wind up stuck all over again, too. You'll put in all that work again just to have the same stress level, the same pay, and the same problems that you've got now.

I could give you my formula right now (or you *could* skip to that part of the book), but it wouldn't work. The take action effect isn't a list of steps and a promise that you'll get rich quick. You've got to start with a take action mindset first, and that's going to take some work to create.

WHAT'S HOLDING YOU DOWN (HINT: IT'S YOU)

The best day of my life came a couple of years after the spying incident when I walked into the office and gave my father's partner my two weeks' notice. It was a small moment in time, but it meant so much. It represented all of the work that my wife and I did to build up to being able to quit—not just building up a business but changing my mindset from one of being trapped to one of taking action.

My father's partner, on the other hand, represented all of the concerns that had kept me there far too long. There were so many reasons to be afraid that day. Although I was leaving the company on not-so-great terms, he had been like a second father figure to me, and I didn't want to let him down. I was definitely afraid of letting my own father down. I was afraid of failing for myself and my family. I was afraid I'd have to come crawling back later, asking for a job.

And then he said the words I'd said to myself too many times: "Are you sure about that? What are you going to do?"

These are the fears that keep us all stuck, right? We don't want to be embarrassed or let people down. We don't know that we actually have what it takes to do something else. We don't want to put our families at risk. We don't want to fail.

TAKE ACTION MOMENT

Yeah, I was terrified—but without this take action moment, I would have stayed in that business (or construction at least) and all of the hours and restrictions that come with it. If I hadn't taken action to pursue this crazy thing my wife and I thought up, I would never have been able to coach my son from T-ball all the way through the age of sixteen. We even got to play a couple of exhibition games at Williamsport, watched the Little League World Series twice, and traveled all over different states to play. I never missed a game, never missed one of my daughter's recitals or plays. Without taking a chance here—without taking action in spite of all the fear—I would have missed it all.

I would have regretted missing those moments that became so important to me. Is there something missing in your life right now that you'll regret in five or ten years? Where are you not taking control of your time or freedom? What is important to you right now that you feel like you're missing out on?

I don't know about you, but I don't want to think I wasted time overthinking things or sitting on the sidelines. So put yourself in your own shoes five or ten years from now—if you find yourself still in the same place then that you're in right now, what will you regret? What could you do, or at least attempt to do, to change that future? This is a take action moment that will affect the rest of your life.

STORIES WE TELL OURSELVES ABOUT OTHERS

Responsibility to other people can feel so heavy. We make a lot of decisions based on what other people are going to think—or at least what we *think* they will think. If your parents have always talked about how you're going to be a lawyer, it's difficult to leave that career. If you start a business with your wife and then discover that you don't like it at all, you don't think you can move on without letting her down. We tend to feel responsibility to the people we work for, too. We feel like they're depending on us, and we worry that if we left we would let them down.

It was so difficult to tell my dad that I was going to quit. Before I put in my notice, I worked up the nerve to talk to my dad first to find out if he'd be okay with it. I felt bad about leaving him with a mess, and I didn't want to let him down. To my surprise, when I told him what I was thinking about doing, I found out that he'd been thinking about leaving, too. Things had gotten so bad that he wanted to give his half to his partner and just walk away from the business and all of its stress. He'd only stayed— get this—because he didn't want to let *me* down. Once it was all out in the open, we were both relieved. Three or four weeks after I left, my father handed over his keys and told his partner good luck.

I can't promise a supportive reaction from the people in your life. They might be like my father's partner—questioning and echoing all of your fears. Or they might completely have your back, like I was fortunate to experience with my father and wife. The only way to know is to get through it. Let the people in your life own their reactions. Don't create a story about them that will just circulate like mental head trash, holding you back and holding you down.

STORIES WE TELL ABOUT OURSELVES

Taking the leap into something that feels really future proof, into something you feel like you can stick with as part of a life that you love, is scary. Whether you're making the first leap into a new business or whether you're already a high six- or seven-figure business owner approaching another pivot, it's not easy. Usually, the fears and insecurities that we have are just more stories we're telling ourselves about who we are and what we're capable of.

With the podcast, listeners contact me all the time to tell me their story. Because I've shared my own story so much, from beginning to end—and all of the thoughts and fears along the way—they tell me that they've gained some perspective. They can see outside of their boxes a little bit and know they're not alone.

Most of our fears are created by our pasts. Our successes often feel like that's all we can do, and our failures feel like we can never try the thing that failed again. Before my current podcast, I tried two other podcasts that didn't go anywhere at all. It was easy to tell myself that it meant

I couldn't do podcasts at all. Before I quit the construction business, it was easy to tell myself that I couldn't do anything but construction. My amazing wife helped me get past both of those fears—first by encouraging our leap from construction into photography (more on that in the next chapter) and later by reminding me that the other two podcasts were missing a key piece (passion and niching down, which we've also got to talk about later).

Can I encourage you in similar ways here?

No matter how big your so-called failures might be or how niched your experience might feel, those things aren't negatives. They definitely aren't a reason to hold back. Each of those negative thoughts can be reversed into something positive.

That pigeon-holed experience you have? It's really just a reliable safety net. Almost twenty years out from construction work, I could still pick it up again if I had to. In fact, I'm confident that I could build a construction business much better than my father and his business partner did. The things that we've done in the past are skillsets that you could use to survive if you had to. Instead of thinking about everything you put in to get to this place (that you now want to escape), think of those things as safety nets.

What about the failures, you ask? (I know you're asking,

because this is the hardest part to let go.) We're going to take failure out of your vocabulary completely. Unless you stop taking action, failure is just experience. There's always something to learn from even the more difficult circumstances. Why didn't it work? What steps along the way were wins and what steps taught you something? The take action effect thrives on that kind of feedback.

When we hang on to failures, they turn into fears that we're going to be embarrassed or that we're going to fall on our faces. So what? I'm not asking you to leave your job right now and go all in, 100 percent, on one thing. It's going to take some time to build this up the right way, and you can do all of that while supporting your family just like you are now. The absolute worst-case scenario is that you'll have to use that safety net. In other words, it's okay to try something and find out it doesn't work. In fact, you have to discover (or rediscover) some curiosity as part of a take action mindset. I'm playing and experimenting all the time until something sticks. Every failure is feedback, and every new thing we try builds on experience to create even more excitement, curiosity, and (eventually) new safety nets. Now I can fall back on construction, photography, product sales, and so much more.

That's part of the secret here: eliminating the concept of failure is how we really become future proof.

TIME TO REFRAME

At first, I was sure that if I could just work a simple, seven-to-three job I would be fine. Then I wanted to just work from home without reporting in to someone every day. I wasn't thinking about impacting people. I wasn't thinking about a business that could provide value to people. Even though some of those things came about, I hadn't even thought about it. I just wanted out of the construction business—out from under that business's thumb and into some freedom.

You're probably looking for some added income or a way out, and that's perfectly normal. But that alone won't get you to a take action mindset. In fact, that tends to be what drives us toward get-rich-quick schemes. It drives the fantasy that we all just want to be on a beach somewhere, sipping margaritas. That'd be fine for a little while (I'm always up for some sunshine and relaxation!) but not forever. Almost all of us picked our careers based on a final destination and a good income, and most of us quickly realized that wasn't enough. There's no way to know from the get-go that you're going to love the career or even that it will still be around in ten years. It's not enough to have a job (and still rely on a few percent raise or a week or two off each year). It's not enough to have a business (and feel scattered and out of control). To really be able to change your mindset and create an action-oriented way of life, you'll need to dig deeper. To get past the thought processes and stories that are keeping you stuck, you'll need to want more.

This is about not missing any more of little Johnny's and Suzie's Little League games and recitals. It's about being at home for bedtime and being free to take off when you want to. It's about being the only person who can tell you when and where you need to be. This isn't a pathway with a destination—it's your vehicle of transportation, no matter where the road leads.

It might be income that you need now, but soon you'll realize you're really looking for freedom, time with your kids, a way to reach a certain demographic, and a resilient business. In the next chapters, we're going to look at exactly what the take action mindset means, the real reason you're here, and how to rediscover what makes you tick.

Throughout this book, I'm going to walk you down the path that I followed from seven bucks an hour and a hard hat all the way to speaking to thousands of people all over the world every day and having the money follow. All along the way, you'll have steps to take, too. Because you need to see it to believe it—more importantly, you need to put it into action to believe that *you can do it, too.*

⚡

TAKE ACTION EXERCISE: TAKE STOCK OF YOUR LIFE

Take a look at your current situation—your trade, business, or career—and ask yourself a few questions:

- How did I get here?

- What about that path drove me to keep going through the training, education, or work that it took to get here?

- What has me feeling stuck?

It's hard to move away from something that took that much work, but look a little bit deeper into the stories you're telling yourself. Are you convinced you don't have the skillset? That you can't waste the time and money it took to get there?

Identify those negative stories so that you can turn them around. For example, "I haven't wasted time or money—I've spent it wisely to get to this point in life, which means I can do it again to get to a place of greater freedom."

RETRAIN YOUR MIND
FOR SUCCESS

Somewhere in between deciding construction wasn't enough and actually finding my way out, I tried a lot of different things. I mentioned in the last chapter that I had been looking for a seven-to-three job, but I was really grasping for anything. I thought maybe I could get another job that had a more predictable schedule, or I could possibly do something on the side to make more money, since money always seems like freedom at first.

My dad always had an entrepreneurial mindset, even while building his company. He'd seen the writing on the wall and was looking for something that would replace the construction business for the both of us, as I would later learn. While still working at the construction company, without realizing that my dad was also trying to escape, I listened closely as he introduced me to Amway.

Amway came with a *plan*. If you aren't familiar or don't remember its heyday, it was one of those multilevel programs where you get people to work underneath you and they get people to work underneath them. Somehow it was not quite a pyramid scheme, though it totally looked like it. But when someone comes up to you and asks you if you'd like to make an extra thousand dollars a month— especially when you're looking for extra money—most of us are going to say *yes*. (Actually I think it's more like *hell yes!*) So yeah, it got my interest.

In fact, it actually made *sense*. People just had to buy the products they'd already use in their own house, as long as they bought them from me. Then, if they signed up, too, they could buy things like laundry detergent from themselves and rack up their own credits. They'd get discounts for using these great products, I'd get something for them signing up under me, and the person who signed me up (in this case, my dad) would get something, too. Then if *they* got more people to do the same thing under them, I'd really be set! Easy. It was going to be awesome.

We were all going to be rich—following the plan and living the life.

As a young guy, that sounded like a great plan. It sounded even better at my first meeting. The whole thing was staged perfectly. People further up in the "upline" of sponsors would show up in their Cadillacs and get paraded around like they were a big deal. We were impressed, too. *Holy crap, these people are successful!* That perceived value was exactly what we wanted to have one day, and the events instilled *the plan* even more into us.

I listened to everything they had to say.

TIME OUT

MLMs are attractive because all we need to do is get behind the existing business model and share it. We don't have to worry about the structure, logistics, sourcing, or anything—it's an instant business. The problem is that it's not *your* business.

As I've built businesses over the past fifteen years, I can see the difference between being a business owner and just being an affiliate, almost an employee, of an MLM. There are pros and cons, like anything, but the biggest one for me is that your business is tied to the main company. If Amway or that supplement or whatever it is you're selling goes under, your business is gone, too.

That model isn't for me, but I learned a lot from my short time at Amway. Maybe you've done the MLM thing, too. If you aren't doing it anymore or you're thinking about stepping away from it, don't think of that venture as a failure. Think about what you've learned and how you can apply those lessons to what you really want to do.

People would tell their stories and everyone would get excited. Just as we were all amped up, they'd tell us what we had to do next: go out and tell everybody you know about this plan and how it can change their lives. They can get better household products, support themselves and their families, and live the lives they want. *Yes!* I bought into it all.

So out I went. I exhausted all of my contacts—which wasn't a lot at the time. Remember this was back before we had email. (We *had* it. We just didn't know what to do with it.) I was literally picking up the phone and calling people, and the only people I could call were friends and family. Since my friends were young guys and not very interested, I started hammering my family.

When I got to my cousins, one in particular stood out. I called her to "catch up" since we hadn't seen each other in a while. "I've got something exciting I want to share with you!" I told her. She said that sounded good and invited me and my wife over for dinner.

Now, this cousin is about ten or twelve years older than me. She knew me as that punk kid who was always getting in the way when she was a teenager. So now that I was all grown up and mature, we were going to sit down for dinner...so I showed up in a suit and tie.

You also should know that I didn't wear suits. Actually,

you should know that I *still don't* wear suits. Maybe to a funeral or a wedding, but that's it. In fact, this suit was one that my dad had bought for me when I was a teenager because we had to go to a funeral.

I'm sure she was wondering what the heck we were doing—and she must have known the second I walked in the door—but she didn't show it. She'd prepared a nice Italian dinner (she was definitely the grown-up cousin, and such a good cook!), and we all sat down to enjoy it. Once we all got done, it was *time*.

"Well, listen," I cleared my throat and began. "I did want to spend time with you. This has been great. But I also really wanted to show you something."

Pause.

I broke out my booklet that had all the details. I went through the entire plan, right there at my cousin's table.

To their credit, my cousin and her husband let me finish the entire presentation, as uncomfortable and awkward as it was. Then they politely told me they weren't interested.

"Really? You don't want to make any additional money? You're happy with where you are?"

I did the whole thing, exactly as I'd been taught. Without saying it, what they really meant was, *We don't want to do to our friends and family what you're doing to us.*

⚡

TAKE ACTION MOMENT

Not every Take Action Moment has a rosy outcome. Some of them turn into something great, and others turn into great lessons. Hey, at least Amway taught me what I *didn't* want! I never *ever* want to chase people for sales again. It might not have been the smoothest action either, but because I was out there trying something and getting results (even awkward ones), I learned something that would eventually shape the way I do sales and business in general.

When I build businesses now, it's deeply ingrained in me to not chase people and instead attract the right people who are interested in what I have to offer. Period. Following this process has made selling almost *easy*. I've figured out how to attract the right people who actually want to purchase from you and your business, and by the end of this book, I'm going to show you how. Don't believe me? Keep reading. We'll get there.

THE STARTING LINE

Mindset isn't a sexy topic—at least not until you really start to understand it. Most of us want to jump right into tactics and strategy. We feel the urgency of our situation and just want to know how to get to someplace better. Believe me, I know. I feel so much excitement and energy when something new is on the horizon for me or anyone else, and I really just want to dive in with you and make stuff happen. But mindset is where my passion really lies, because I believe it changed my life.

Here's the truth: true success is all in your head. Or at least mostly. Anyone who has found success will tell you that it's about 80 percent mindset and 20 percent tactics and strategy. Having the right mindset means you're always learning and growing, you're always building that mindset like a muscle. The minute you let negative thoughts in, it's like staying on the couch instead of going to the gym. Your mindset muscle will wither away, and you'll slip right back to where you were.

Back then, on the heels of that dinner, I didn't know much about mindset at all. I didn't realize how much my own mindset had been altered by that experience. I was embarrassed. I quit Amway with my tail between my legs—afraid to try anything else without looking like I was hopping on get-rich-quick money schemes. I could picture my friends and family rolling their eyes. "There goes Scott again..." "Oh, it's Scott. I don't want to pick up the phone..." "Scott's just going to show me another thing..."

Even though I still wanted something more than the construction business could offer, I stopped looking for a while. I went back to my job. I went back to thinking it was all I could do. My mindset had already been low, with fear and doubts, and now it was even lower thanks to embarrassment and a little bit of hopelessness.

I couldn't dwell on it, though, or I'd slip toward depression. Here I was, in my early twenties with an incredible wife and a job that paid the bills. In fact, she was able to stay home with our kids. What else did I really need? I couldn't let myself dwell on disappointment when this was obviously where I was meant to be. My father was a hard worker and so was his father before him, so that had to be who I was, too. I was meant to be a hard worker who does whatever is necessary to take care of my family.

When I thought about having more freedom, being an entrepreneur, or making more money, I pushed it aside. Amway had gotten me excited—we're talking over-the-moon excited—that I might possibly be able to pull off a low six-figure income with some control over my life. Then just like that, Amway reminded me of what I really believed: that kind of life had to be for other people. Smarter people. Not me.

It wasn't until about a year later, when my mother-in-law got rid of some Tony Robbins cassettes, that my mindset started to turn around again. She had already listened to them and just wanted me to donate them for her, but before I passed them along, I popped one into the player. It was the *Awaken the Giant Within* series, where Tony talks all about getting clear on who you are and where you want to go.

He talked about how one thing that felt embarrassing can't stop you from doing anything for yourself. He talked about doing things in life that are uncomfortable, and using them to learn to do what you want and don't want out of life. He said you can't just throw in the towel after you try something once and it doesn't work.

Man, that hit close to home.

I wasn't quite a believer in everything Tony Robbins had to say, but it was too relevant to ignore. As I kept listening, I learned that the things I'd been thinking about myself and my potential weren't real. They were products of how I'd been taught. I learned that we actually *can* have whatever we want. Here was Tony Robbins, this person who is recognized as successful in his space, telling me that I could do incredible things with my life, and I started to get the sense that he was right. Without actually experiencing it, without making a dollar outside of working for my father, I started to see the potential. I soon realized how *good* I felt with those encouraging messages in my head.

My mindset was slowly starting to shift.

NOT ALL BAD

The only guarantee I can make in this book is that if you try nothing, you'll get nothing. I can't promise that taking action will bring a good result—but I can tell you that your mindset will change the way you think about that result. That's why you have to start with mindset before anything else.

Looking back with this newfound, growing positive perspective, my Amway experience hadn't been all bad. It put me in public places with lots of people and taught me how to network. Getting comfortable in those spaces helps me to this day, and so does what I learned from some of the books they had me read. *How to Win Friends and Influence People* changed the way I felt about interacting with people in general, especially while selling. It taught me to sell myself rather than my product and to always genuinely care about people—to help them rather than sell to them.

The big lightbulb moment came when I realized I could take those lessons and apply them into the next thing, whatever that thing might be. For instance, I knew I wanted to figure out a way for people to come to me rather than me chasing them down. I wanted to educate people and build trust with people who found me and wanted what I had to offer. I wanted to be a resource rather than an annoyance.

No matter what you do—even if it's right on target and ridiculously successful—you're going to doubt yourself. No matter what you do—even if it's breaking out a sales booklet at your cousin's dinner table—you're going to learn something. As long as you take the action and push through the discomfort, something usable will come from it.

Depending on how hard the lesson was, you might have to take a break after the worst of it, too. I felt like I was running back into my comfort zone, and in many ways I was. But since then I've noticed that I still tend to take breaks to reset. I'll play in a new environment or model to see if I like it, and then I step back when I find that I don't like something. With a little distance and some time to reboot, it's easier to figure out what I learned from that experience and how I can apply it in the future.

A break is different than running, though, and if I could shake younger Scott's shoulders to tell him that, I would. I'd tell him not to give up. I'd tell him life doesn't have to be so limiting, and that if he'd just keep going—keep taking action, keep pursuing what he really wants—he could have it. No one in my life was doing that for me at the time. Of course, if they had, I wouldn't have all the stories I'm sharing with you. My learning curve would have been cut significantly shorter. Yours still can be.

YOUR ADAPTABLE BRAIN

The mind is the number one driver for results, and its number one goal is to protect the body. New, uncomfortable experiences look like danger—except when we can see someone else who's already been there, done that, made the mistakes, and proved that nothing bad actually happened to them. With someone to follow and model after, suddenly it's not so threatening and dangerous.

Fortunately, we live in an amazing time. We can model successful people in almost any scenario. Whatever you want to do, wherever you are, there's someone who has been there and is going where you want to go. Model their lifestyle, learn from their mistakes, and shortcut your own process. Let their mindset becomes yours, even when you don't quite believe it yet yourself.

It's easier than ever to get the right messages and get in the right mindset, but it's just as easy to model ourselves after the wrong mindset. If you hang around people who are always complaining, convinced that online businesses are scams, don't believe any of this will work—guess what you'll believe? It won't even be intentional. That's just what a steady brain-diet will do. If you were to eat nothing but garbage, you'd feel like garbage (and probably look like it, too).

To create the life you deserve, you have to create a new

mindset. The thing you're working on now might not be the thing you're working on in five or ten years, but the mindset work is going to last. Don't worry about figuring out the entire path from here to there. Instead, we're going to work on small changes that will allow the take action effect to happen. That means clearing out some mindset blocks that have likely been in your way.

TIME OUT

Before we take a look at these mindset blocks, remember that it's okay if you have some (or all) of them. We all do. These fears, habits, and mindsets are there to protect us. At the same time, it's important to face them and push through them so that you can achieve your full potential. So that you can get to that groundbreaking Take Action Moment that will become part of your incredible story.

MINDSET BLOCK: FEAR

Yes, the mind protects us from danger, but we can and do consciously create the stories that determine what danger actually is. For example, if I jump off a cliff, I could die. That's real danger. But if I try to launch a business, it might not work as planned. If I grow an email list, maybe no one on it will buy from me. Those things aren't dangerous at all—in fact, they are great opportunities to get information.

The next time you feel fear creeping in, ask yourself,

"What's the worst that could happen?" If I try this thing and it doesn't work, I'm probably not going to die. That's good. So what's the real risk?

When I left the construction job, I was scared. But what was the worst that could happen? I'd have to fall back to my safety net. It wouldn't be ideal, but it would be safe. When I started my most recent podcast, it could have failed like my other two, but I wasn't hinging my family's budget on it. My other businesses kept me safe. What's your safety net?

Train your mind to look at each attempt or venture as an experience. Once you learn how to reframe your fear, you can face it and take action.

MINDSET BLOCK: SELF-SABOTAGE

After Amway, it was all too easy to think of the ways things could go wrong. Specifically, I thought of all the ways I wasn't good enough to achieve my goals. Often, we decide not to try at all so that we definitely won't fail. We make excuses about why this thing won't work for us. We procrastinate and stay put in order to stay safe.

Teach your mind some kinder thoughts about yourself by thinking about past experiences that went well. Why were you great at that thing? I bet you even struggled at times, but you kept going. What got you to the finish line? How did you win? Play those stories over in your mind. Think about times when you were fearful but went ahead anyway and achieved your goal. Get rid of the negative stories and replace them with positive ones.

This next step is harder, but it's powerful: look at negative experiences. Think about times where you didn't win, even if it's awkward or painful. Ask yourself what you learned from that situation. Even at Amway, I learned basic sales skills. I learned what I didn't want. What were the positive takeaways in your experiences?

MINDSET BLOCK: OVERWHELM

Being future proof doesn't mean knowing exactly what the future holds and how you'll respond. So many people want to know that everything works before they ever get started. I heard a quote once that said, "If you wait for all the lights to be green you'll never leave your driveway." This is so true. Looking too far ahead is a mistake. It takes your focus off the small steps in front of you and makes the whole thing feel overwhelming. It's suddenly too much work, too much to learn, too many unknowns. So you stop and never do anything.

A friend of mine wanted to start an online business, and he was still in the early stages. I told him he needed to figure out a market first and then go to YouTube to find other channels that were doing what he wanted to do. Then I told him to randomly shoot five videos and post them, not expecting anything to happen. Three steps, low pressure, that was it.

About four weeks later, I followed up with him and asked how he was doing. He said, "Well, I haven't done anything yet."

"Why not?"

"I haven't figured out how to edit the video."

"Uh...you mean the video you haven't shot yet?"

He didn't need to edit the video if he hadn't shot it, and he didn't need to shoot it if he hadn't found a channel, and he couldn't find a channel without picking a market. Why on earth would something four steps away stop you from taking the very first step at all? Trying to figure it all out first gets people stuck. It's overwhelming, and it keeps them from taking action.

If you're building a house, you don't start by figuring out how to get the shingles on the roof. That comes so much later in the process. You've got to start by digging the footings or laying the foundation. My friend Pat Flynn from Smart Passive Income taught me a long time ago to practice something called "just-in-time learning." Learn only what you need to know when you need to know it. Don't worry about the future right now. You'll get there. There are too many steps ahead of you yet to worry about the shingles now. Chunk your big goals down into small steps, and don't worry about what comes next.

THE POWER OF POSITIVE

One of my students and a member of my private Inner Circle group started out with a full-time job in IT. A few years ago, he didn't necessarily want to leave that job, but because it was in the corporate world where downsizing was a real risk, he wanted to create a new safety net by starting something on the side.

This was all new territory for him, so he faced a lot of doubt and fear getting started. He pushed through those fears and decided to take action anyway, using Amazon as his platform and building a business on the side. Two years after he got started, the company that he worked for in IT did decide to downsize after all. Fortunately, his "side business" was generating a six-figure income. He's now living on his new business, 100 percent, without any problems with being downsized.

The catch is, as you grow, new fears and doubts will arise.

His current concern is that Amazon is his only channel—what happens if it goes away? He's now focusing on growing his business through digital marketing outside of Amazon, and he's pushing himself to grow and learn and move forward in his journey. It's normal to be afraid. Just acknowledge it as a part of growth.

The right mindset keeps you motivated. It's often driven by your "why," which we're going to talk about in the next chapter, and it ensures you'll do whatever it takes to get there. You'll push yourself even when you don't feel like showing up, because your mind isn't focused on the negative. It's looking for the positive, the potential, and the purpose in what you're doing.

A positive mindset doesn't have to be a fearless mindset. In the face of fears, though, you can avoid "garbage in, garbage out" responses by surrounding yourself with like-minded, positive people. Get close to forward thinkers who will push you to the next level.

In my own life, my wife has been a tremendous source of encouragement and positive mindset. She's one of my biggest motivators and cheerleaders. This year, we're celebrating our twenty-fifth anniversary of marriage and raising our three awesome kids as I write this book. Without her introducing the idea of a photography business, the take action effect in my life would have looked entirely different.

There's one moment in my life that I'm so grateful happened. It all started before I turned twenty-one, at the end of a long day of work, when my buddies wanted me to go out with them. It just sounded like too much hassle. I was tired, and I was just sure I would wind up left outside waiting while they all had fun. They said they knew the bouncers at the bar we were going to, though, and they insisted it was going to be great. I still felt pretty "meh" about it, but they managed to drag me off the couch, and I went.

Little did I know that my someday-to-be wife was on a couch in her part of town, wanting to stay in after a bad breakup. Her girlfriend dragged her out, my buddies got me out, and somehow we found each other in the same club on that one night when neither of us wanted to be there in the first place. For twenty-five years, we've done everything together. She's not only my life partner and my business partner but my biggest supporter. If I'd listened to the voice in my head that night and stayed in, I never would have met her, and who knows where I'd be today? I might have been coerced into action that night, but I'm so thankful I was!

Tony Robbins introduced me to personal development and the concept of surrounding yourself with like-minded people. Pat Flynn has been someone that I model after not only for his approach to business but because he's a family guy as well. He taught me how to chunk big things down into smaller tasks to avoid becoming overwhelmed (which I often feel). I've never been a big reader, but I've learned how—starting with cassette tapes and now, thankfully, audiobooks. The older I get, the more power

I see in reading and absorbing information to apply in your life.

Sometimes surrounding yourself with positive influences means creating some space between yourself and negative influences. That can be difficult. People whom we love and admire can be negative influences that we might have to filter out. If they're family, it's even more difficult. Creating space might look like limiting time around them or training your brain to sort out what they have to say. Your mindset is worth protecting, though, even when it's challenging to do so.

THE TRUTH ABOUT DISCOMFORT

Although the horribly uncomfortable dinner table sales pitch taught me that I didn't want to do cold calls anymore, especially to family and friends, it took some time and a mindset shift to really understand that. At first, I just wanted to get away from the discomfort. I ran right back to my comfort zone in my dad's business. I went back to telling myself that wanting more than what I had was a pipe dream. I went back to the messages that society and school had taught me, that the only way to get a six-figure income is with the college degree I didn't have. Those limiting beliefs were embedded deep in my mindset, and it was easy to go back to them. It was comfortable.

If you want to make a change in your life, business, or job, you have to have a different mindset than the average person. I'm living proof. If I'd accepted the norm, I would still be in the construction business—miserable, with low self-esteem, living paycheck to paycheck. I would have missed games and recitals and plays, and I would have been kicking myself for not pushing past the discomfort.

I still find myself shying away from discomfort. It's completely natural. I'll dread retreats when I'm not completely familiar with the environment, even when I know they'll be great for me. Or on a larger scale, I'll worry about launching something new when it might not succeed. In those moments, the easy choice is to talk ourselves out of it. After all, our minds and bodies know that sometimes discomfort or pain is a signal to step away. I wouldn't really recommend cold-calling family members and blindsiding them after dinner. Part of my discomfort probably signaled a problem with that scenario. The in-person retreats and the podcast, however, needed to happen no matter how fearful or uncomfortable I was.

So how do you tell the difference?

I can't give you any hard-and-fast rules. You're the only one who can dig deep into your mindset. Ask yourself what you're really afraid of. What's the worst that could happen? Then, here's the kicker: spend some time thinking about what might happen if you let yourself bail. What might you miss out on? How much will you regret it? Is this a take action moment that could change everything? Will it carry a lesson you need to learn?

The take action mindset will always lean into good, productive, growth-signaling discomfort. Stretch that muscle and build it up. You're going to need it for the work we're about to do.

TAKE ACTION EXERCISE: STORYTELLING

Take Action Moments happen at all stages of life. Just the other day, I watched one unfold for my eleven-year-old daughter. The night before a volleyball tryout, she started to complain about being nauseous and not wanting to go. Even though she'd been playing on the twelve-year-old regional team at eleven years old and the tryout was a formality, she was still really nervous. In fact, she almost backed out completely. My wife and I reminded her of how great she was at volleyball and all she'd accomplished before, and encouraged her to go in there and give it a try. Just as we'd thought, fifteen minutes into the tryout, they told her she'd made it and didn't have to finish that day or come back to the second round. She was definitely on the team. Now she'll have a whole season with new friends, and who knows what direction it'll take her life, all because she took action.

- It's time to give yourself some credit where credit is due. What have you done in spite of being afraid? You faced your fear and accomplished what you thought was impossible.

- Now think about when you tried something, but it didn't work out as planned. What did you learn from that experience?

Think as far back as you need to—you'll be surprised at the stories you can tell. These are take action moments, where they either open new doors or teach you new lessons. Stopping the negative stories and instead looking for take action moments is a powerful way to prove to yourself that you can keep going, no matter the immediate outcome.

DISCOVER YOUR HIDDEN SUPERPOWER

When I was working construction, I didn't get to see my kids much. I'd give my little daughter a kiss and tuck her into bed at night, snuggling up next to her as she drifted off to sleep. "Goodnight sweetheart. I love you."

From the doorway, my wife would recall something adorable that happened earlier, before going to take care of our infant son in the other room. I was so grateful that she could be at home with our kids all day, catching all of the little things that children do as they grow up and explore the world.

I'd lay there, taking in every moment I could with my little girl, trying not to transfer the dried paint and sweat covering my skin and clothes I'd worn all day at work onto her as we cuddled. I was so extremely tired that I'd usually drift off to sleep as she did, not waking until one or two in the morning. Then I would jump in the shower, sleep just a little bit longer, and start my day all over again before she was up in the morning. Day after day, missing moments and milestones, it all started to wear on me.

Family has always been important to me, and even more at that stage of life. Having a child of my own caused me to reflect on my own childhood, and I knew I wanted more quality time with my daughter than my mom had with me.

My mother was fifty years old when we lost her to a heart attack, and her short life was full of struggle. Her childhood had been marked by an alcoholic father and abuses that she kept buried for most of her life. As an adult, pregnant with me, she and my father lived with her parents, while my dad was in the navy. One night my father heard a heart-wrenching scream and ran downstairs to see what was wrong. It was my grandmother, who found my grandfather in the garage after he took his own life. That moment would forever change my mother's life. Her trauma showed up as deep depression, which she self-medicated with prescription drugs and alcohol, just as she'd been taught.

She was also a strong, loving woman who modeled openness and vulnerability. She never hid her darkness from us kids, though for years I wasn't sure why she would go away for weeks at a time, or stay in her room in the dark. As I got older, I'd learn that she was cycling through bouts of rehab when she was gone and when she came home and got clean, without the alcohol to help her battle her demons, the depression would take over again.

I'd try to sit with her in the dark, not sure why she was so sad. I just wanted to be near my mom.

Sometimes she'd let me stay home from school, because she didn't want to be alone. Fifth grade was difficult for me to pass because I missed so much school. Sixth grade was even harder because I understood a little bit more about what was happening, and I couldn't pay attention to my classes. I just wanted to get home—*what if she's gone again before I get there?* Every day leaving school, I'd dread looking for our car. If it wasn't there, there was a chance she was off to rehab again, which I was so afraid of. I remember that she gave me twenty-five cents to take to school, just in case I needed to call her on lunch to make sure she was still there. I did use it on the very first day of school, because I needed to hear her voice.

In spite of having a supportive dad and an open mom who taught me so much that makes me who I am today, my childhood wasn't easy. My parents fought in front of us kids, and I'd pray every night that my parents wouldn't get a divorce. When that day finally came to be, my mom sat me down on the corner of her bed and told me what I'd been dreading to hear: "Scotty, your father and I love each other, but we just don't think we can live together anymore."

Then, she asked me something I hadn't anticipated: "Who do you want to live with?"

Anxiety bubbled up inside of me again as I told her, "I'm going to stay with whoever has the house." I wanted my parents together, but what I needed was stability. My mother understood and ultimately knew that it was the right choice. She never questioned, never made us feel guilty. She moved about ten minutes away, and my father helped her get on her feet. He was always so good to her, in spite of their relationship. She was able to focus on rehab, and for twenty years she stayed completely sober before she passed.

She adored us kids and did her best to show us. She taught us how to be open and never shove anything under the rug. She was the parent I went to in high school when I got serious about girls. My dad would give me the "supposed to" answers, a little bit more strict and rule-based, but my mom would give me honesty. She'd tell me when something was a bad idea but also help me stay safe if I was going to make that choice anyway. I could be completely open with her, without any judgment.

She was a ton of fun, too. She'd play outside on the slip and slide or jump on my dirt bike to take a ride. She'd just be a kid with us—and with my kids. My daughter remembers her as "the funny one," the one who would crawl around on the floor and play peekaboo or chase her and be silly. She even had the chance to hold my son a few times before she passed. I know if she was still here, she would have loved my kids to the fullest.

The day she passed, I was completely in shock. I mean, I'd just lost my mother. But at the same time, I couldn't help feeling some sense of relief for her. I had watched her struggle my entire childhood, and in a strange way, I felt she was finally able to rest.

TIME OUT

This part of my story is bittersweet. I don't want my mom to be viewed in a negative light at all, and I don't want you to feel sorry for me. Right down to my mom's sense of humor showing up in me and in my youngest daughter, my childhood made me who I am today. I'm so grateful for it all.

A lot of us went through difficult times in our childhood, though, and you might be able to relate. If you had times in your life that tested you, try to reframe it. What kind of person did that make you become? What did you learn from it? What did it help you achieve? Instead of hanging on to the negative, think about what you've pulled out of those challenges. Believe in yourself and who you've become in spite of the hard times.

Do I wish it had gone differently? Do I wish that they'd stayed married and she'd stayed alive and we'd all had our happily ever after? Absolutely. But that's not how our script was written.

My script, on the other hand—the one with my beautiful wife and children—that one was still in progress. I had some control over it, and there was nothing I wanted more than for my kids to have a different story to tell. I wanted to feel rooted and for them to always be safe and loved in our home. I wanted to be close to my family as much as possible. I wanted to create a home where my kids wouldn't be afraid that one of their parents would be away for long periods of time, like I used to worry about as a kid.

Ironically, I was working so hard at my father's business so that I could create that stable home—but in the process, I was losing touch with my kids. I would still go out and swing a hammer if that's what I needed to do in order to create that safe, stable home for them. But what I slowly came to realize was that the money and the home weren't my real motivation. It was my relationship with my kids that kept me going. I wanted my kids to feel like I was there for them no matter what. I wanted them to brag about how much I was there for them. How much I did for them and how much I spent time with them. I'd been operating as though I could only make enough money to support them was by working more. But if I continued down the road I was on, I would continue to miss out on that relationship.

My kids were my *why*, and that's what gave me the superhero strength I needed to push past fears and doubts to create the life I really wanted.

STOP—READ THIS FIRST

I know you want to skip this first part—of identifying your own why—and get to the "good stuff," but this is important. You can't just scribble down a surface-level answer and move on. There really isn't a place to go from here if you don't get a why in place first.

Honestly, I didn't know how to say *entrepreneur*, let alone spell it, when I started to get a handle on my why. I had no idea where I was going, and it wasn't important right then. All I knew was that I needed freedom and flexibility to be with my family, and working for myself could make that happen. There wasn't a moment where I woke up and knew where I was going and why, but it built up over time. The more I craved time with my kids, the harder I wanted to work to figure something out.

Trying to leave the construction business took a lot of extra work on top of being overworked and exhausted. My *why* made it possible. What was an extra six or eight months of sleeplessness in the face of a lifetime with my kids? I was obsessed with making something work. Sometimes, I'd put a ton of effort into something that wouldn't work at all. Thanks to my why, I had much more resilience than I did during the Amway fiasco. I might be dissuaded for a day but nothing could make me quit. *All right, fine. Slide that attempt over and let's move on to the next one.*

Life isn't always easy, which is why we have to start with the right mindset to create a frame that will carry us through each chapter of our lives. There are going to be ups and downs and times when you feel like giving up. If you get through it and reach that goal, something else will show up on its heels. It always does.

The last day I worked for my father was the first day I

committed to a full-time business—it was on November 1, and I'll never forget it—I felt like I won the lottery.

I hadn't arrived, of course. Your *why* isn't static. It's not a goal that you reach and move on from. Like Tony Robbins says, if you're not growing, you're dying. The take action life is always moving toward something new, and the only way you'll have the fuel to get through it all is to have a clear why.

When you feel like giving up, when it seems like everything has failed, you'll always have the why to come back to. Before you leave this chapter, you're going to figure out what that is.

IT'S NOT WHAT YOU THINK

Your why is not going to be what you assume it is right now. Even by saying "my why is my kids," you're not going deep enough. Your why isn't going to be a sense of hustle for the sake of hustle, either. You can't force yourself through this effort.

There have been times where a lot of work was necessary—not as much sleep, working through lunch breaks, and skipping dinner with friends. The constant grind is not my end goal, though. If it's yours, go for it. I personally don't want to work sixteen hours a day and sacrifice years of my children's lives just to say I hustled. I want a lifestyle business. I will put pressure on myself, and I'll probably kick your butt a little bit when you start to drag your feet, but it will always be in a positive way. I'm not beating myself or any of my people down.

Sometimes that external, positive pressure can even look like your why. I've been very open about the fact that I will never work for another person again in my life. Not ever. That's a powerful claim! When you make a statement like that, you've got to own it. If you declare to someone that every morning you are going to do a hundred pushups, and for every day that you don't you'll pay that person a hundred bucks, they're going to hold you to it. But don't let it fool you—external pressure isn't your superpower. That's not what will make you future proof.

When you don't feel like getting up early in the morning to work on your business before your nine-to-five starts, it won't be a to-do list or someone else's words that get you out of bed. You're going to be thinking about that big payoff that you want so deeply. When people walk through the exercise we're going to do to find your why, it often brings them to tears. We're digging far enough to wake something up inside of you on an emotional level. That deep-seated emotion is what pushes us further than anyone else can, taking us past our fears and supporting that take action mindset.

HOW TO FIND YOUR (REAL) WHY

The first thing to figure out before you can dig into your why is your motivation. Everyone's motivation is different, and you'll need to find your own. Understanding these different types of motivation can help you stay the course. Maybe you need some praise along the way and you need to surround yourself with positive people on a regular basis to help push you forward. Maybe you need to see small improvements along the way to prove you can do it. These can be drivers that help keep you motivated and encouraged to keep going when things get hard.

For me, I'm not motivated by material things. Short-term wins or victories are different than long-term motivation. If you're interested in the take action effect, you're probably a lot like me. Money is just money. The helpful thing about money is that it allows us to do the things we really want to do. So maybe money does motivate you, but before you settle on a "number" as your why, make sure you look closely at what you want to do with that money. That's probably pointing you toward your real why.

Your why has to matter. It has to be something real that means something to you on a deep level, or you won't be able to use it as your drive.

To do this exercise right, you have to be willing to open your heart. Dive deep into your core and trust the process.

Don't underestimate the questions. They are simple but powerful. When you ask yourself these questions, you're going to get answers as long as you're being honest with yourself.

You also need to do it on paper, away from any sort of screen. Whenever we put things on paper, especially with ink, it feels tangible. It's real. It's permanent. You can't effectively do this exercise on a computer or phone. Even when you have notifications and an internet connection turned off, there are still visual distractions on a screen that you don't get when you step into a quiet place with a notebook and pen.

Take yourself away from all distractions and give yourself the time and silence to really answer these questions. Once you get into the flow of these topics, you won't want to break it. You don't want someone coming in and interrupting you and breaking your focus. Let your family know that you need a little bit of time—in fact, trade time with your partner. Do the exercise separately, and then come together to share what you came up with. It might turn out to be very similar, and then you can keep each other accountable. Sharing with someone who doesn't naturally judge you can make it feel even more tangible, real, and achievable.

You can do this exercise to dig into any sort of motivation, not just for a business or working for yourself, and you can do this exercise multiple times throughout your life. Any time you're facing a decision or wondering what you need to do, you can revisit these questions to check in with yourself. It won't take long, and once you've done it you'll have it forever. You're going to write it down and keep it somewhere that you'll see it all the time, because you need to remember why you're pushing yourself.

SEVEN WHYS TO FIND YOUR WHY

The exercise starts with a single question. It will be different for everyone, like "Why do I want to leave my job?" or "Why do I want to build a business?" or "What does my business need?" The question needs to get you talking about what you want to achieve. From there, you're going to ask yourself "Why?" for every answer you give, about seven times over. The answers you give will be driving deeper and deeper until you get to the core of your motivation. Your ultimate why.

When you say you want to leave your job *because you want to be home with your kids more.* That's good. Keep going. Why do you want to be home with your kids more? *To see them grow up.* Oh. There's a little bit of emotion in that, isn't there? You'd probably even elaborate without asking the next why. *I don't even want to think about not watching them grow up. I'd feel bad. I'd feel like I missed something important.* Keep going—keep asking yourself why until you get to the seventh why. That's where you'll get to the heart of what you're doing and why.

I'll give you an example in my own life, looking back at leaving my construction job.

1. What do you want to achieve? *I want to leave my sixty-hour-per-week job.*
2. Why do you want to leave your job? *I want to spend more time with my family.*
3. Why do you want to spend more time with your family? *I want to be a huge part of their lives.*
4. Why do you want to be a huge part of their lives? *I want us to enjoy time together...and for them to remember me as a good father and husband.*
5. Why do you want them to remember you as a good father? *I want to be a role model. I want to show them stability through my choices in life.*
6. Why do you want to show them stability? *I want to lead by example so they have what I didn't. So they see that they have choices and can be in control of their lives.*
7. Why do you want them to be in control of their lives? *Because time is precious and we all deserve to be happy and enjoy every moment.*
8. Why is life so precious that we should do what we enjoy? *Because I never want to live with regret.*

There it is. I'm creating a business and leaving my construction job so that I can spend time with my family and never regret not taking the time to enjoy our precious moments together.

GETTING DOWN TO THE NITTY-GRITTY

This exercise is powerful because it gets past the superficial goals and down to the emotions. It gets to the core reason that we're doing something. A lot of people want to jump in with "I want to make a lot of money" or even "I want to make a lot of money so I can be free." Why, though? Those surface-level reasons aren't really it. Keep asking yourself why until you uncover some deep emotion.

To really get to the heart of your why, go back in time. In mine, I started to travel back in time to my childhood. I remembered what it felt like when my father missed a baseball game. I remembered summer vacations where I had to have a babysitter while he worked. I felt it all over again, and I knew I didn't want my children to have those feelings and memories in their own life. Think about what brought you to this point and what created the feelings that you have. What made this thing so important in your life?

When you uncover your why down to these deep, personal, historical things, you'll have it forever. You'll feel more connected with your thoughts from then on. I know that when something for my business conflicts with my kids' events, it's very important that I prioritize my kids. Missing a special moment or time with my kids is not even an option. I know exactly what I need to do—they always take precedence.

Now I keep a note next to a picture of my family. It says, "I will create my lifestyle business so I can set my own schedule and never miss time with my family." That image is in front of me when I wake up, and it's there when I go to bed. It's always in front of me, reminding me of my why. Whenever I'm feeling down or frustrated, I can look at that note and the faces of my wife and kids and remember what I'm actually doing.

When I started the podcast, I went through the seven whys all over again to combat the doubts I was experiencing. It took me from wanting to help people start their own business or escape their nine-to-five to the feeling of helping someone change their life to helping them believe in themselves the way I didn't for so long. Ultimately, I wanted my kids and others to remember me as someone who served and inspired others. My kids are almost always at the root of the things I do, even when it's not immediately obvious.

Taking some time to identify my why always reminds me of my ultimate purpose and what's really driving me. When my podcast theme clearly needed to pivot from Amazon sales to business building, I was worried about my listeners losing interest. Then my why kicked in. If I didn't keep going—if I didn't share what I'd learned to model success for my listeners—I definitely wouldn't reach the people who needed that message. I couldn't affect their lives in a positive way.

Keep your why close to you—you might even want it to be in several places, like your screensaver, a paper in your wallet, or a note on your mirror. Put a reminder wherever you need some motivation. It can serve as your personal motivation. It can be the foundation of your business's mission statement. It can interrupt feelings of defeat. It can keep you focused. Now and then, run through those seven questions again. Remind yourself of where you're going and why—because that's your hidden super strength. It's the engine behind the take action effect. Now we just have to figure out where you're going.

TAKE ACTION EXERCISE:
CONSTANT REMINDERS

If you haven't already, walk through the seven whys. Start by asking yourself, "What do I want to achieve?" Maybe you want to grow your existing business or start something new. Maybe you want to leave your job. Maybe you want to make $10,000 a month, or grow your business from $10,000 in monthly revenue to $50,000. These are all great goals to have, but the number really has to do with your *true* why. The money just allows you to achieve and enjoy your why.

Tips: Imagine that I'm in the room with you, asking you these questions. Dedicate a full hour in a room by yourself, without any screens or distractions at all. Use a pen and paper or notebook—you're inking this stuff to make it real.

DREAM BIG (AND MAKE THEM COME TRUE)

Until you can let go of your self-limitations and dream big, you won't be able to make it to your real dream and your real *why*.

Now, I'll offer a disclaimer here. If you're dreaming of going to the moon (and you don't already work for NASA), your odds aren't so great. Not many people in the history of the world have stepped foot on the moon. So we'll say that the literal sky is your limit. Everything else, though, is achievable. Hundreds of thousands of people have gone before you, building businesses and working from home. Even better than that, hundreds of thousands of people have made six and seven figures online—more than enough to make your *why* your reality.

When I left the construction business, I thought I'd hit the moon already. I couldn't believe I was working from home, enjoying life with my family. My wife and I worked up to the point where we were doing really well in that business. We were taking our kids to and from school. We were at all of their games. By all of those original standards that I'd dreamed of meeting, we had it made.

But we weren't quite free. Not really.

Our business was in photography, which isn't exactly hands off. (Yes, I know—you still want to know how we made the jump from construction to photography. We're getting there, I promise.) All of those client appointments and shooting sessions quickly started to feel like a job again. We were committed to shooting at certain times of day when the lighting was right, we had to do follow-up appointments, take stuff to the lab, package it all up...The thing we hadn't realized was that working for ourselves wasn't the only key to freedom. We also had to stop trading time for dollars.

Although we thought we knew what our perfect day was, we hadn't let ourselves dream big enough. All I'd wanted to do was set my own schedule and make $75k or so. While it felt like a big dream at the time, I've learned since that it was limiting. There is no ceiling to what we can make and achieve. We simply have to decide what we want and then go out there and get it.

⚡
TAKE ACTION MOMENT

My photography business is ultimately what introduced me to digital marketing, and trying to figure out digital marketing led me to my first purchase of an online course. That training program was $2,000 way back then, which I had to put on a credit card and hope I could pay it back before the interest came due. During the course, I had the opportunity to get on the phone with its creator, kind of like a business coach. He asked me, "What do you want to make per month that would make your life what you want it to be?"

I thought I was being so big and bad when I threw my number at him: "I'd want to make $15,000 a month."

But he just chuckled.

"That's great," he said. "I thought you were going to say something a little bit larger than that. This won't be a problem at all." He went on to explain that in the online space, if you even half try, you should be able to double that. He told me that he was hoping I'd say at least $30,000 a month. "But it's okay," he reassured me. "We'll start there."

That one conversation—that came from that one course that I could barely even pay for—changed the way I think, even to this day. I thought I was stretching myself, but I wasn't even close. Our potential really is limitless.

ENTER THE BIG VISION

My wife and I started slow, poking around at the possibilities that might be out there. We had no idea what exactly was available to us online, but we knew there was *something* out there. We didn't have any specifics, and that's okay. Instead of trying to map out a path to a specific opportunity or business, we just asked ourselves what it would look like to keep our time and still support our family.

With a solid grasp on our why and self-permission to dream without limits, we decided to make something similar to a vision board. (You guessed it—another exercise is coming!)

Now, let me be completely clear on this: a vision board is not something you create and then expect that the stuff on it will magically appear. That's not the point. It's more like me talking to you about riding an elephant, and suddenly you can't stop yourself from picturing the experience of riding an elephant. Admit it: you're thinking about it right now!

I'm going to assume you've never ridden an elephant before, but there you are, perched up high on an elephant, doing whatever it is one does from up there. (I wonder how good the sound quality for a podcast would be...) The cool thing is, if you want to go out and ride an elephant, you could possibly—even probably—make that happen. Even cooler? If you want to make the things on your vision board happen, there's almost no doubt that you can.

I know this sounds like the law of attraction, which says

when you think about something, the universe will bring it to you. You may or may not believe in that, but I can tell you one thing is absolutely fact: if you focus on something, you'll start to see it everywhere. I bet you've already experienced that in your own life. Have you ever decided to get a car that not a lot of people have? It seems so rare and special...until you start looking for it. Suddenly, it's on every corner. Why is that? People didn't rush out to buy the car that you wanted. They'd always been there—you just hadn't paid attention to them before.

We keep our heads down through most of life now. Thanks to social media, we don't pay attention to what's happening around us. We don't see any details, we don't hear the birds chirping, we don't feel the wind blowing. We're just so distracted. A vision board gets you clear on what you want and plants those images into your head. It brings your vision into your day-to-day life. You can see what you actually want. You're reminded of why you're doing what you're doing.

Together, my wife and I started to dream about the perfect day (no limits!) and what that might look like. Then we gathered images and clips of what that day might look like and put it all into a video slideshow—one for her and one for me. It's one thing to write down words or talk about what you want out of life. It's another thing entirely to see them in pictures. Images make things feel real.

We both included a Disney cruise. While we were doing well and providing for our family, a cruise seemed like the height of luxury. Sure, we could afford little trips down to Florida to stay at my father's and hop over to Disney for the day, but there's no way we could drop $6,000 on a cruise. That's something we wanted to do for our family, so into the slideshow it went.

Mine also included a picture of a beautiful breakfast out on a back patio, with the sun shining and healthy food on the plate. I added some exercise equipment because I wanted to be healthier and in shape. There was another image with a person sitting in their home office, sipping a cup of coffee, that represented my dream of working online. I was tired of showing up to appointments every single time I needed to make a dollar.

It wasn't all business, either. I added guitars, too! I'd been in a band growing up, and I missed playing. I also added a Mustang muscle car.

When I was sixteen, my father loaned me $3,000 to get a car. Not just any car either—a 1985, four-cylinder Mustang. I'd always wanted my own car, especially the fast, eight-cylinder Mustang that I really wanted. With my father's help, I got the Mustang I could afford and souped it up. I loved that car. Then, when I turned seventeen and got that seven-dollars-an-hour job with the cable company (heck, I thought I was living large!) I replaced that car with a 1987 Mustang GT—my very first muscle car. It wasn't long before I had to grow up. Once I became a father and husband, I had other responsibilities. I decided to sell that car to help me make improvements on our small, two-bedroom starter home. I never stopped loving those cars, but I needed to do the more grown-up thing and support my new family.

My Mustang was more than just a car—it gave me the feeling of freedom when I drove it with the roof open. It was also something that I achieved as a young man and gave me a sense of accomplishment. I had set my mind to it, and I got it. So my video had to include a Mustang that I'd hopefully one day reunite with.

You can see, though, that our vision board video wasn't about partying, Lamborghinis, and extravagance. We just wanted to visualize a life that included things that we really wanted to have and do. What did we want to achieve? How did we want to spend our time? As part of our morning routine, we watched our videos...for a while, anyway. We probably watched them off and on for six months and then fell off the wagon—not unlike what we all tend to do with exercising or starting a new habit. But that little bit of time planted a seed. It embedded in our minds exactly what we were working toward. It was a constant reminder of the life we could have if we just kept taking action. It was a piece of the take action effect, before I even knew what it was.

Two years later, I looked around on the deck of our Disney cruise and suddenly remembered the videos that we'd stopped watching months before. It hadn't come to mind during the booking process or leading up to the day we left port. But when I was actually there, sitting next to family and my father and stepmother, it brought back the images I'd put into the video. It had burned into my brain, and I eventually made it happen. That's the power of the vision board, and it's why we have to dream without limits.

DREAMING IN TECHNICOLOR

I'm going to ask you to do something that might be difficult. I want you to write down exactly what you would want out of life if there were no limits at all. You don't have to worry about how it will happen. Wave the magic wand and trust that it will come true. (Okay, get out of the rocket—everything short of going to the moon. You know what I'm talking about here.) You have to allow yourself to think bigger than you ever have before and then put that down on paper. Remember how paper makes things feel real? That makes this exercise feel really uncomfortable at first, but it's worth it.

Going back to my photography days, I would have loved

to show up, take pictures, hand everything off to an editor, and then have someone else who did the viewing, someone who set appointments—all of it. If you can relate, maybe you would wave the wand and people would appear to run things in your business; that will give you some of your freedom back.

Do you want to start a business but don't know how? Wave the magic wand. If you could do anything at all every day, what would it be? Cut out pictures. Jot down notes. Picture what it would actually look like. What motivates and excites you?

While I do believe the universe is listening to these things, I know without a doubt that this exercise changes your mindset and the way you think. When we want to make something happen—something specific and clear and connected to our why—we do everything we can to make it work. So even though you don't have a plan now, just thinking about it and picturing it makes it much more likely that we'll figure out the plan later. That's why we're spending so much time on mindset before tactics. Having the right mindset, a clear why, and an inspiring vision in place makes the tools that much more effective later.

THE PERFECT DAY

It might be a little bit broad to think about what you could do if you could do anything, so let's break it down. Strip away everything you don't know how to do, everything you're wondering about what comes next. From the time you get up in the morning to the time you go to bed at night, what do you want to do in a normal Monday to Friday week?

If you're already a business owner, a good first step might be to envision getting everything done within that week instead of working through the weekend. Most of the time, people who are working nine to five take the weekends off and then dread going back on Monday, while business owners work nonstop and dream of making it a nine-to-five schedule. There are always trade-offs and pros and cons, which is why I don't want you to worry about the "how" at all. Let's just picture that perfect weekday. I'll start with mine.

> I love mornings, so I'd like to wake up bright and early before everyone else. Let's call it 5:30 a.m. As soon as I get up, I'll splash a little water on my face, brush my teeth, and do fifteen minutes of meditation. I can just imagine how amazing I'll feel after that. That'll get me ready to walk to my gym, which will be either in the basement or garage. I'll put in a thirty-minute workout that will make me feel strong and like I've done something good for my body. By then, my kids will be up and getting ready. I'll spend some time with them as their morning starts and then take them to school.

When I get back, I'll take a walk with my wife and then sit out by the pool to have breakfast with her as the morning starts to warm up. Around 9:00, I'll start work—with the stuff that I genuinely want to work on coming first. These are the tasks that don't feel like work at all, so I want to keep that great morning going by tackling them first. It's okay that I don't know exactly what they are right now.

I've always liked to work in blocks, so I'll take a fifteen-minute break for every hour that I work, up until about 12:30, when it's time to have lunch with my wife. For an hour or an hour and a half, she and I will enjoy lunch together, until I go back to my office to do another block or two of work. That's when the business gets shut off for the day, and I go to pick my kids up from school and then enjoy the day as it comes. We might go to volleyball practice or take a long walk with the dog or the kids. Everything from here out will be leisure and not work.

Dinner will be all together as a family, where everyone gets to talk about their day. We'll hear what everyone is excited about or challenged by and then settle into something together as a family for the evening. After the kids go to bed, I'll shut my night down with my journal, some reading, or an audiobook that will get me in the right state of mind for bedtime, which will happen at a decent time. When I wake up the next day, I'll be refreshed from a great night's sleep and ready to do it all over again.

Sounds great, right? Did you see some of my old vision board stuff seeping in? To be honest with you, that's kind of what my life looks like right now. That's what I wanted, and that's what I went out and built.

My challenge to you is to make your own perfect day. I didn't know exactly what kind of work I'd love to do or how I'd manage to work a few hours each day and then enjoy the rest of my time with my family. It didn't matter that I didn't know how. If you can't quite give yourself permission to dream this big, let me do it for you: you are free to dream.

WHAT'S HOLDING YOU BACK

When we chase the money and the "how," it becomes too overwhelming to pursue. All you're thinking about is how far away that dream feels. I'm not saying you'll write it out and it'll appear. But without knowing where you're headed, it'll be a whole lot harder to stay focused on the journey to get there.

If you don't have a vision, you won't see the opportunities. It becomes a self-fulfilling prophecy. Of course you can never reach what you don't admit exists! In part 2 of this book, we're going to uncover so many opportunities for you that you probably didn't know were possible. Before we can do that, you have to admit to yourself that the things that are out there can be for you, too.

If you let yourself envision the perfect day, then you give yourself permission to pursue it. You admit that there is a chance that day could be yours. Then you can take little actions here and there, which turn into results, and the take action effect takes over. Twiddling your thumbs isn't taking action. Wishing and hoping isn't taking action. But a clear vision backed by a strong why can really change things.

THE TAKE ACTION MINDSET

If you haven't caught on to what's happening here, flip back to the chapter on mindset. Dreaming about the future (and dreaming big) is a new exercise for most of us. Remember, the brain treats new things like something dangerous, and we have to do a lot of work to teach it new habits.

Self-sabotage is a big mindset block that shows up when we try to dream big. We convince ourselves that we don't really want that kind of success. What would we do if we had it, anyway? That kind of thing is for other people, right? Wrong. Those thought patterns are self-sabotage, and they show up when we start going for something we've never experienced before.

Once, I read about a guy whose mother had raised him to believe money was bad. People who have money are greedy snobs, she taught him. Well, he went on to become pretty successful, but he had some bad habits. Every time he'd make a lot of money, he'd lose it somehow. For a long time, he didn't know why. He'd keep making money and then losing it, over and over again. I don't know if it was through therapy or something else, but he eventually realized that his subconscious messages about people with money being bad were taking over. He was self-sabotaging an otherwise successful life.

The other mindset block that shows up here is overwhelm. Remember my friend who couldn't even pick a market because he didn't know how to edit videos yet? His story is so common. Lots of people limit themselves, thinking they can't possibly have breakfast by the pool every morning because they don't know how they're going to make the money in the first place. Forget the how. The how is coming, but not until we do this first.

Right now, we've got to figure out the lifestyle we actually want—what is it that we want to withstand whatever the future has for us? What are we fighting for? What are we creating and protecting? This work that we're doing to create a take action mindset is a whole challenge in itself. Doing the work to make it happen is something else entirely. Work on one before the other. Hijack that sense of overwhelm by doing one thing at a time.

With that in mind, I want you to keep reading, even if you don't feel like your take action mindset is totally solid yet. We don't have to have everything perfect. Remember, these are muscles that we're developing, and it's going to take time. Thoughts of self-sabotage, fear, and overwhelm will show up over and over again. If you don't move until they're completely gone, you'll never get anywhere at all. Take what you've learned in this part of the book and layer it over the next steps as you learn them.

The steps I'm going to lay out are ones that I've repeated over and over again in my career, and I continue to use them any time I build something new. Eventually, it's like muscle memory. I don't even have to think about it anymore. Mindset, a strong why, and a clear vision take a little more effort. If you do the work to keep those pieces in great shape, the rest is going to fall into place.

TAKE ACTION EXERCISE: DREAM BIG

I don't have a slideshow or a vision board anymore, but I still write my goals down. I have notebooks full of lots of things that I'm working toward over the quarter or for a year, and I go back to reference them. I've also got posters all over my office—massive forty-by-forty canvases with reminders like "Remember Why You Started" and "Stop thinking about it: just do it!"

No matter how you do it, when you write something down it becomes real. At least in your subconscious mind. So break out the markers and glue, or iMovie, or a PowerPoint. Find a way to turn your perfect day into a vision board. Connecting images to our dreams changes the way we view the world. You don't just want $3,000—you want that Mustang. You don't just want an income, so what is it that you really do want?

You have my permission to dream big, but that's not what you really need. You need to give yourself permission. Do you have that? Good. Now—ready, set, dream!

PART 2

BUILDING YOUR FUTURE-PROOF BUSINESS

DISCOVER A FUTURE-PROOF YOU

There are some moments in your life that you just don't forget. One of mine happened in the corner of a formal living room that I hardly ever used. It was furnished with a couch we never sat on and a gifted TV that didn't work. I sat in a wooden chair in the corner of that room, still wearing my worn-out work jeans, thumbing through the newspaper classified ads like I'd done for weeks on end, when my wife sat down across from me.

"What are you looking for?" she asked me.

"I'm looking for...something else. Something where I can just work from seven to three and come home to see you and the kids. I'm tired of getting up early and coming home late. I'm tired of not seeing you guys."

All I wanted was some stability and a little bit of time with my family, and all I knew how to do was work hard for someone else. I'd already been burned by sales attempts, and I thought there wasn't anything else I could do but work. I was a construction worker. That was it.

My wife saw things differently. She told me, "You need to do something other than just working with your hands. There's *something* in you that you can do."

"Yeah, well, I don't know what that something is."

To my surprise (and disbelief), she did. Sort of.

TIME OUT

What I'm about to share with you is an absolutely *huge* turning point in my life. The thing is, I didn't even know it at the time. This day would forever change my life and lead me to building and owning multiple businesses years later. This was a Take Action Moment and *the* take action effect in full force.

Okay, are you paying attention? Good. Back to how my wife came up with an idea that would change our lives *forever*...

My wife had watched a segment on *Oprah* that got her thinking about doing things you're passionate about and that will be fulfilling. She's always had a love for photography, but she never took it seriously at all. It's funny, because most of her pictures were taken on a disposable camera, but people would always comment on how awesome they were.

She reminded me of our recent Easter photos with the kids, where a local studio offered a free eight-by-ten photo for scheduling a photo session. It had real live lambs that created a unique and amazing set that would create a beautiful portrait. The studio offered a free eight-by-ten as part of its marketing and then sold my in-laws and my wife three hundred bucks in prints.

I remember giving my wife a hard time, because at the time we couldn't afford it. We wanted the free prints and that was *it*. There wasn't any budget room for anything else. But that $300 we spent on pictures would end up being a huge part of helping to build a six-figure business a few years later, all because of that single day and that *Oprah* show.

Here was her big idea: she suggested we start our own photography business. She reminded me how stressful it was at the photography studio getting our kids' pictures taken but how people were lined up to pay hundreds of dollars for pictures of their kids. She was convinced we could do a better job in our local area, which means those people would line up for us.

Of course, neither of us knew how to do photography at all. Sure, Oprah said it was a good idea, but how could we really turn a basic interest into a business?

"Don't you have to go to college for that?" I asked her. My own self-limitations were still going loud and clear.

"I don't think so. I think you just have to be good at it."

I looked down at the classified ads and then back at her and said..."Well, all right, then. Let's give it a shot. What do we have to lose?"

Keep in mind this was back before digital cameras and YouTube videos were a thing, and we had no idea what we were doing. We also had no idea how much of an investment it would be to just "try it." So, with about $3,500 charged on a credit card, we got a Nikon F90 and a professional lens, a backdrop, and two umbrella lights. We also bought a couple of books on lighting and portrait photography and then dove in.

When I wasn't working, we were adjusting lights and camera settings, taking test photos, and running them to the one-hour photo lab to get them developed. Then we'd compare the photos to the notes we'd taken about each of them and figure out what we needed to change to get it right. It was time-consuming and expensive, but we stuck with it. A few months later, we'd have our own ad running in the local *Pennysaver*, offering free four-by-six prints with a Christmas photo shoot.

We started out by offering free four-by-six prints and then grew by word of mouth. By the second year, heading into Christmas photos again, we'd built up some momentum and we had some local buzz. It felt like a great side business to me, but again my wife had caught the bigger vision.

"I think you need to quit your job."

I'm sorry, what now?

"I think you need to quit. I'm not going to be able to handle the customers that we're building up to, and I need you home for this to really work. We need to just go for it. What's the worst that could happen—you'll have to find some side work? That's not a big deal. Let's do this."

That was two weeks before November 1, which you'll recall was my first day of freedom. It's another moment in time that I'll never, ever forget. I came downstairs that morning, passed that little wooden chair in the corner of the still-unused room, and brewed myself a cup of coffee. No one was tracking my time. No one was expecting me to do anything that day. *Holy crap. I'm free.*

I picked up my mug and stared out the back window. The sun was already up and I was still at home.

Holy crap, I thought again. *I hope this actually works.*

YOU'RE NOT A ONE-TRICK PONY

I was scared as hell, and all I could think was that this had to work. It had to last. Sure, I could go do some construction side work if I needed to. I had enough skills for it, and there was a competitor in town who would have loved to have me work for him. So there was that safety net still technically in my back pocket. But that's not what I wanted. I wanted this to work out. If it didn't last into the future, I'd be right back to the stuff I'd wanted to leave.

That Christmas season was really successful. Our goal was to bank $10,000 to carry us through the off-season, and sure enough, we needed it. There were times when we lived week to week, charging bills to a card while things were slow and then paying it off when we got busy again. The back and forth was constant, but we made it work. I was living the dream.

Oh and just to be clear, if I had to write down what I did on a W-2, it'd look like this:

> Scott makes silly faces and jumps up and down to make kids smile.

Yep. That's it. And for a long time, that was plenty. I was working for myself, taking care of my family, and loving it. Mostly. Eventually, I realized what Oprah had been saying was true. I needed something that fulfilled me. Lisa was able to make these amazing images that families took home as keepsakes. We were a team—our sessions were so much more relaxing and enjoyable than what I remembered of that Easter session that started it all. When people booked sessions, they were coming for us. "Always get Scott and Lisa" became the local mantra. We weren't just selling our photos; we were selling the experience and environment that we created. If I had to jump up and down and make silly faces to create our unique selling proposition work, then that was my contribution.

Hang on. Selling proposition? Maybe that's it...

As soon as I started figuring out marketing, it had my attention. My job started to shift into getting more people in the door so that the off-season wasn't so difficult. I got excited about marketing and the challenge of bringing in customers. I started to build an email list by gathering info every time someone would come into our studio. Whenever we ran a special, I'd send out an email and we'd book up within just a couple of days. For example, we had people coming in dressed for Christmas sessions as early as August.

The more I learned about marketing, the more I discovered about online businesses. With every new action I took, I got a new result and learned a little bit more about myself and my potential and what's out there. I started to light up again. I was uncovering my own passion and discovering things I enjoyed. I loved getting attention, bringing people in the door, and giving them an incredible experience.

It wasn't scary to try new things anymore. For the rest of this book, I'll walk you through the take action effect snowball that carried me from photography to eBay to digital sales to education to where I am today. I still had that construction work safety net, but I wasn't worried about falling back on it anymore. Now I had all of these other nets, too, and I wasn't dreading any of them.

TIME OUT

Listen, I don't want this book to be all about me, but rather about you discovering your take action moments and the effects from acting on them. Usually, opportunities become clearer the more that you experience different things throughout your journey. Think of my stories as a chance to gain some experience you might not have yet. As you are reading this book, reflect my stories and, later, my listeners' stories against your own. If you can turn what you're seeing and learning into action, who knows? My ultimate goal is for this book to become a Take Action Moment in your life that helps you achieve your own goals and dreams.

PASSION DRIVES THE TRAIN

My *why* motivated me to take the leap and try something new with my wife. My mindset kept me in the game even when that first off-season in our photography business came and sales slowed down. But it wasn't until I aligned it all with my passion that things really took off.

At first, I thought photography had to be successful in order for the whole thing to work. That was still the tape playing in my head: you pick a thing and you stick with it forever. But that's not what it means to be future proof. We can't make a job or a business stick around. Instead, we've got to figure out what will make *us* stick around. What's keeping us lit up and excited and curious?

That's really the most important thing you need to

know—and what's great is you don't even need to know it right away. Forget about making money or unlocking some hidden vault of passion. What's one thing you'd be excited about waking up to do every day? Take some time with that. We'll spend time doing internal research and exploring the possibilities, because you're not jumping into this right away. You can build this up on the side and play around until something feels great. When you find it, that passion will drive the train that takes your business to places you haven't even dreamed of yet.

If you're not sure yet, a great place to start is with the things people always ask you about. We've all got something, and you don't even have to be happy about it. In my next life, I hope I don't have to be handy again. If you're handy, people always want you to fix stuff for them. (I can't tell you how many weekend decks I've built over the years! Someone asks if you can *help* them build the deck, and then you end up building the whole thing for them. It's a blessing and a curse; what can I say?) In any case, it's a thing you can do. That's a start.

We're not used to thinking about what we can do, much less what we want to do. We think about what will make money. What will be a "good job." What lines up with the degree or trade we chose. Most of us spent years going for that six-figure job or a business that would strike gold. We didn't think about what got us excited and if that thing had an angle that served a market out there. I can promise you, the things you're interested in have a market, and you can serve that market just by showing up as your excited, passionate self. That market might not always be your target, but that's okay. It's not what's future proof. *You* are.

⚡

TAKE ACTION MOMENT

Notice how I didn't wait to find my passion in order to get started? I was too tired, too worn down to know what I was really passionate about right then. In fact, I'd say I didn't hit my actual passion point until *The Amazing Seller* podcast in the last few years. I jumped into photography with my wife because of the life that I could see it making for us. Passion is great, but don't put this off until you've found it. If I'd waited around at the construction site to find my passion, I never would have left.

In the same vein, we can't wait for credentials either. The cool thing about that is results become their own credentials. You might not have a background in teaching people how to fish, but if you teach Robbie to catch more fish, he's going to look at you as an authority anyway. When you and Robbie talk about that weekend when he caught more fish, other people will look at you as an authority, too. In other words: *taking action* is the only thing that will get you past your fears, doubts, and hang-ups.

MAPPING OUT A FUTURE-PROOF PLAN

All this about mindset and theories are nice, but it can still be hard to imagine yourself actually doing it. I've asked you to put off the "how" for a while now, and I know you're ready to figure it out. Don't worry—you don't have to learn a brand-new trade (unless you really want to), and I promise the take action effect isn't about chasing every shiny thing that comes your way. There's a method to my madness, and it's a method that just about anyone can follow.

Generally, the people who listen in on my podcast or come to me for coaching are in one of two camps, and if you're still reading this book I'd bet you are, too.

CAMP #1

There's the person who's stuck in their nine-to-five job or corporate life who is just sick and tired of it. They've been there forever, usually have grown up in that company or industry, and now they feel stuck in that spot. Although they'd love to be able to do something they really enjoy, they have no idea how to actually make that happen. Believe it or not, the steps I'll lay out for you can help you discover hidden talents and passion you might've forgotten you have and then apply these principles to create a plan for the future. You'll use that take action mindset and turn it into a take action effect that will keep you going even when things don't work like you'd planned. Even when you're doubting yourself. You'll come back to these steps (probably to see where I was when I hit a similar wall) and figure out the next thing you can do to keep on moving forward.

CAMP #2

Then there's the existing business owner. If you're in this camp, you probably had an easier time with the mindset chapters. You already know what it's like to take the leap into the unknown and work hard to build something new. What's bothering you is that the whole thing has lost its spark. Now that the thing is built, it's not as exciting as it was. You're left with what feels like a boring job again or, maybe worse, a monster that's spiraling out of control and taking over your life. What you really need is a roadmap that will help you figure out exactly what to do next so that eventually you can turn this thing around—or maybe turn it into something else entirely.

The steps we'll take over the next few chapters happen one at a time, no matter which camp you're in, and then build toward the next step. By the time you get to the end, your business is ready to grow and expand almost naturally. It's a framework that you can apply to any new business, venture, pivot, or product.

It goes like this: first, you have to identify a market. We've started to think about that possibility already, and in chapter 6 you're going to find one for yourself or get clarity in your current one. Without a clear market, there's no point in trying to sell any product or opportunity. Don't worry about what you're going to offer just yet—all you'll have to do is find something you love to do or are good at and then find someone who's interested in it, too.

Then, you'll need to get their attention. You'll figure out where your market hangs out and what it is those people need and then start offering them value. The goal here is just for them to see who you are and what you can help them with to get results in advance of the sale. This isn't about the product or offer itself yet—and you'll see in chapter 7 why that's so important to remember.

Next, you'll be able to build a bond and a relationship with them. On YouTube that looks like subscribers, on Facebook it's a like or a group member, on Pinterest it's a follower, and so on. You can only build a bond by offering value to that person on a regular basis. That's what chapter 8 is all about. It's helping them on their journey, and for some of them, that journey will lead to the last part: sales.

The moment you've all been waiting for is still several chapters away, because the sales I'm going to talk about in chapter 9 are only easy when you've done the work leading up to it. When we've got the attention of the right, niched down market and have built a bond with them that allows us to contact them and follow up, the second they need what we have to offer, we won't have to wait to build trust or get through a certain number of "nos" or anything else we're taught about sales. It'll be a natural decision for them.

A STUDY IN SUCCULENTS

I want to share a story about a friend of mine that has created a very successful business around a super niche market: *succulents*. The thing that she was interested in was niched down perfectly from the start: she loved succulents. She happened to be a freelance photographer who did a lot of product photography, so she combined her skills and background with her interest and started a blog about growing succulents.

For several months, she put up a post a week without getting much traffic at all. It was just something she enjoyed doing. Not long after, she realized that her website was starting to get more traffic and decided to install Google Analytics to track some of that traffic to see where it might be coming from. Once she started learning more about traffic, she started to learn about search engine optimization (SEO) to see what that whole thing was about. Then she learned about searchable long-tail keywords and started to add them into her posts.

Traffic picked up a little bit more, though she was still just writing a post a week, so she added Google AdSense, to monetize her traffic to her blog just to see what might happen. The very first month, she made a hundred bucks. This blew her away and fueled her to keep going.

For a while, she kept working on the same things, until she had a good amount of blog posts. By this point, she knew her market pretty well—and she knew they still needed more information. So she compiled a bunch of her blog posts and turned them into a pretty, small, *helpful* e-book. When that launched, she sold about a thousand dollars' worth. Now, she was ecstatic. There was no stopping her.

Even though some months it seemed like the traffic was low, she kept going. She did the same stuff over and over again, always following her interests and being helpful to her market, no matter what. It's been five years now, and her little succulents blog gets 350,000–500,000 unique visitors a month. She's making more than six figures a year from ad networks and her e-books, and her husband is a full-time stay-at-home dad.

There wasn't any magic involved here. She showed up to something she was passionate about, found a *market* for it, learned how to get that market's *attention*, offered consistent value until there was a *bond* in place, and then made some easy *sales and continues to.*

Now, I know what I just described might sound foreign, like SEO or AdSense, but I'll explain it as we go. It will all make sense later, I promise. If your mindset is in place, your why is in hand, and your vision is clear—it's time. Let's take some actions.

⚡

TAKE ACTION EXERCISE: VALIDATE YOUR PASSION

If you're in Camp #1: What hobbies or interests came to mind as you read through this chapter? Without limiting yourself at all, think about what you're interested in, what people ask you about all the time, or what you get excited about. Now go to YouTube and search for that thing. Let's say it's bass fishing. You could run a search for bass fishing and see what can be found. Did something come up? There's your validation: your interest *does* have a market. In the next chapter, we'll niche that down to something more specific.

If you're in Camp #2: If you have a current business and you are not sure who your market is, you need to figure that out. This is critical, and the framework I'll be sharing will need to know who your market is. Do the same exercise as above—search on YouTube and see what your market is posting about, or if you can find a clear sub-market. You may also find that your market is too broad and you need to niche it down. Everything I'll be sharing in this book can be applied to an existing business that will allow it to grow and generate more revenue.

To see examples of this process, go to TakeActionEffect. com/Bonus.

MARKET DISCOVERY

Every successful business, pivot, or product that I've gone after has followed the process we're walking through right now. Even when I didn't realize it. Back at the photography studio, we took my wife's interest and found a market for it. We got that market's attention first by offering our services at a discount and then by delivering an excellent experience. Over time, I learned how to build an ongoing relationship with those clients by building up an email list and staying in touch with them, offering them specials and letting them know when it was time to book an appointment. Eventually, that made the sales come easily, and we got past those off-season dead spots.

We did get there, but we had to learn something by experience that I'm going to teach you in this chapter: finding a market isn't the same as niching down into the *right* market. You might already own a business, which means you've found a market. But are you really happy with it? Are you still excited about it? Is it reaching the exact right people?

Since our business was already in place, we had to do some experimentation to niche down. We did a few weddings at first—that made the most sense. If you're a photographer, you shoot weddings, right? Nope. Wrong. Uh-uh. Weddings are *stressful*. They are chaotic, and there's so much pressure on you to capture all the right moments in just the right way. Shooting weddings took away the creative outlet that my wife enjoyed about the business, which really took the wind out of the sails for the whole business.

We kept trying to find a niche—bar mitzvahs, anniversaries...nothing seemed quite right.

And then there was Anne Geddes.

That style was at its peak. Newborn photos were all about the baby lying on the father's arm, the elaborate backdrops, the Victorian washbasins and flowers everywhere. Now we had it. We knew where we wanted to focus and could really start to get our name out there.

With a clear, specific market to get in front of, I had to

learn how to get people in the door—which would ultimately become my focus and shift my life's path.

CHASING PASSION

Believe it or not, I used to say I'd never own a computer in my life. My father had one, and I thought they were completely useless. Actually, it was less the computer that annoyed me and more my father. He was on that thing all the time, not even with internet on it. He was just doing work for his own side businesses, and I thought it took up time without any benefit. I thought it was a waste and I didn't want anything to do with it.

It didn't take long for me to change my tune once I saw what people were able to do with them. When we started up the photography studio, we asked a friend to make a price list for us, and I was blown away. She made it on a PC/Windows machine, and since my father was always a Windows guy, we went out and got a Windows computer and a website building software, Dreamweaver, to help build our business. After a little bit of a learning curve, I made us a website for the photography business. (And, naturally, my father has never let me live it down.)

A little while later, a friend of mine who did some design work told me, "You've got to get a Mac. The graphics are so much better, and it runs Photoshop better, too."

Photoshop?

We'd worked so hard to learn how to take great photos because we had one shot. There was no post-processing or retouching involved. We had to take great pictures that came out reliably, and that was it. In fact, we'd even invested in hand-painted backdrops and set designs that cost two to four thousand dollars each. Our studio was full of unique props like French washbasins and elaborate, Anne Geddes–style accessories.

Photoshop was a game changer, in more ways than I realized at that moment. I got my first iMac (a blue one!) and ordered a Photoshop 6 Bible—it came with a CD and everything. I was so excited to get started that I had the book shipped to my father's place down in Florida so that I could read it while we were on vacation.

As soon as it came in, I sat down on the couch and cracked that four-inch-thick volume open. It's funny, because I opened that book years later to find a picture that my daughter drew, that I used as a bookmark while I pored over the content throughout that trip. (D for Dad on the front, a whole bunch of Xs and Os, and the note *I love you, love, Alexis.* She's twenty-three now, and I still have the picture stuck in the book.) When I got home, I started applying what I'd read from the book so it would really sink in. I'm not much of a reader, but that was probably the best $64.99 I've ever spent in my life. That book probably led to seven figures or more thanks to the lessons I learned in it.

The book taught me everything I needed to know to be able to edit pictures for clients, but I turned it into so much more. I started creating templates for customers so that we could offer things like baby announcements and Christmas cards. Soon, we were making templates all the time, and then we expanded into digital backdrops, which drove our first course I ever sold. Needless to say, the guy who didn't want to own a computer had become a Mac guy for life, and some take action momentum had been set in motion.

GET SPECIFIC—FOR YOUR BENEFIT AND THEIRS

We'd initially found an okay market in our photography studio. Our offer was that we could make the photography experience enjoyable, while still creating amazing portraits for families. But the photography itself was just another job for me. I still had to work more hours to make more money, and nothing about the actual process meant anything to me personally as far as passion goes.

Finding that unique angle—gorgeous, Anne Geddes–style photos—and figuring out how to sell it, on the other hand, had sparked a passion in me. Suddenly, I wanted to learn and try all that I could. Getting Photoshop, playing with new techniques, offering new services, and exploring the potential on eBay were all ways I could find what someone needed and provide it for them. So I kept taking new actions and measuring the results.

Then, there was eBay.

We'd heard a lot about people going to garage sales and buying things to sell at higher prices on eBay, so my wife and I spent some time exploring different categories to see what was out there. After we saw what eBay was and how quickly you could sell things, my wife came across some little landscaping cedar bridges that looked familiar. Keep in mind we were always looking for new unique photo props for our studio. When she stumbled on a little four-foot, $30 wooden garden bridge at our local Christmas Tree Shop downtown, she remembered seeing them on eBay for $130 while looking for props.

Out of curiosity, she bought one, brought it home, listed it on eBay, and two hours later we had a bid. Sure enough, it sold for $130.

What?

The day after the listing closed, we drove back to the Christmas Tree Shop and loaded the minivan up. With all the seats down (and a couple bridges strapped to the roof) we took every last bridge they had—fifteen to be exact—and went home to get them listed on eBay. Those things wound up paying for our kids' tuition that year, at a time when we couldn't pack any more sessions or work into our schedules. Selling stuff online seemed to be the way to make more money without having to work (too many) more hours.

If eBay worked so well for bridges, what else did I have that I could list? My clients enjoyed the holiday templates I made, so I decided to list a couple of them to see how they'd do. Soon, I was selling five or six templates a week—an extra hundred bucks or so without much effort at all. We were blown away and excited about this extra revenue.

After hanging out in photography forums, I soon realized there were other photographers out there getting started just like we did. Fortunately, we were able to buy all of the backdrops and sets that we needed, but it would have been nice to not have to all the time. Many of the people I was reading about were even more limited on space but had a budget for high-quality props and backgrounds. I wondered...could we have people take their client pictures on a green screen and then edit our backdrops in? That could be more accessible than spending a couple grand on hand-painted sets.

So I shot a bunch of our expensive sets and props as templates and listed them on eBay as well. I was right—those did well, too. Now we had not only a set of great products but a name for ourselves. I could help people get started doing photography without all of the expenses—I could help them do exactly what I'd done to that point.

What *had* I done to that point? My answer to that question was a lot more confident than it had been a couple of years before that. Without any training or degrees or experience, my wife and I started a photography business with $3,500 and some patience (and a whole lot of trips back and forth from one-hour photo). Then we turned it into something full-time and fun. This time, instead of hearing all of the what-ifs and self-doubt that I had told myself for years, my mindset had shifted: *I can probably share with people how we did that.*

SHARE IN THE JOURNEY

YouTube had picked up steam by that point, so I started a little channel just to share my experience. On a short, awkward video—my first one ever—I told my story and then let people know that they could ask me any questions they had. And they did. A little audience started to form, and we would get feedback and questions and spend time communicating with the people who were watching.

From all of these sources, I built a little email list of about five hundred people, and I started to learn what I could about email marketing. I set up a follow-up sequence in Outlook mail, and I let them know when I had something new. From what I was learning about marketing, I knew that if I just kept offering them value, then when I sent them something to purchase, there's a good chance that they'd be interested and would eventually buy.

NICHING DOWN LOOKS DIFFERENT FOR EVERYBODY

Let's look at my process again: I enjoyed marketing our photography business. Then I realized people could use the templates I'd learned to make. Then I realized that there were other photographers like me who could use the sets we'd built. Then I realized those same photographers could benefit from my journey. After we made it down the photography business, my continued process of niching down took me from a budding interest in marketing all the way to educating new, DIY photographers who wanted to start and grow their businesses like I'd grown ours. Those were the people I needed to get in front of.

Here are some examples of others who have found their niche and built businesses that allowed them to go full time.

CASSIDY

We've already talked about my good friend who combined her interest in succulents with her photography skills. When she got tired of the basic jobs she'd been doing for photography clients, she directed some of that energy into a fun blog. She didn't really know if she could turn it into a business, but she enjoyed documenting things as she grew succulents. The homework she did to make a better blog led her to SEO, and a few months later, traffic started to trickle in. She put ads up as well, and when she made a few dollars on that she realized what the potential might be if she brought more traffic in.

As time went on, she expanded into affiliate marketing

and then e-books, and now she's launching a small course. It's only thirty dollars, but she easily sold two hundred of them before the launch was over. She started with something she loved, validated the market by putting the content out there and seeing what traffic she could get, and then built it from there. She gets over 500,000 uniques a month, making well over six figures a year, and all of that without even launching a physical product (yet!).

TIME OUT

Something interesting about anyone who has built a site or a blog and generated traffic—now you understand how to build sites from scratch and get them ranked. These skills can be applied to any market and niche, especially when you know how to validate the market before you even start. When you're constantly taking action and learning, you're always adding to your skills and creating more options for yourself!

LOUIE

A listener on my podcast had a couple of hobbies that eventually intersected. He liked making websites but hadn't figured out something that would make him much money. Just for fun, he enjoyed bass fishing. At a local bait shop, he connected with a championship bass fisherman who'd been making bass fishing lures. This guy really knew what he was doing—wrote for top magazines and won tournaments—and when he'd put the lures for sale on Craigslist, they'd sell out every time.

When my buddy realized the opportunity here, he had a thought: "What if we put these online and see what happens? I know about marketing, and while I love bass fishing, I'm not an expert. What if we partner?" Together, they launched a successful online brand selling from Amazon, selling on their own website, and publishing content on a regular basis. People learn from them on Google searches, through their email list, and by finding their videos on YouTube. Together, they were able to find a niche that neither of them could reach on their own.

DAVID

Another example comes from a friend of mine, David Young, who found a great niche pretty quickly. Like a lot of people, when he was younger, he went to college just because everyone else did. But what he really wanted was to be a pilot. Eventually he did make it to pilot school— only to realize he was afraid of heights. So he became an accountant. As a CPA, he threw his name in the hat for a long-shot job at the FBI just to see what happened, and he got it. He never lost his interest in flying, though, and eventually got interested in flying drones. When he realized you needed to pass certain exams to get a permit to fly drones, he thought he could help people get through that complicated process. He put up a website, drove a little bit of paid traffic to it, and did well selling that service.

The problem came when that exam became obsolete. His business had to shift right away—so he pivoted. Instead of teaching people how to pass the exam, he sorted through their processes for different licenses and airspace that you needed to pass other exams. Within about a year and a half, he was able to quit his job and go full-time with his drone school. Not only did he teach people how to start flying, but he also showed roofers how to use drones for inspections and real estate agents how to use them for pictures and video. He's currently working on a course to teach people how to make $1,000 a month flying drones for those people. By constantly pivoting, he's been able to keep growing his business until he was doing what he wanted way back before he became an accountant.

ALEX

Finally, there's Alex, who was a listener on the podcast and is now a good friend of mine. She was a digital nomad, which is someone who intentionally doesn't have a home. Usually a digital nomad is young, in their twenties or thirties, and they backpack around the world, sometimes meeting up in groups or clans to hang out as they travel and work. Alex just wanted to enjoy traveling, and she found that there wasn't a good resource online for women to learn about packing lighter or best practices for traveling. She heard about people blogging and making money while doing it, so about six years ago, she started to blog about her travel experiences. Every few days, she'd show up on her blog with a new article, learning more about SEO as she went.

Things took a twist when she wasn't much of a digital nomad anymore. Instead of stopping, she niched further down and started writing to women about fashion and traveling light. Now, her brand is Travel Fashion Girl. Thanks to six years of content that has built up a ton of traffic, she gets over a million unique visitors every month, which she uses to create monthly revenue from. Once she realized what her top affiliate sales were, she started private labeling products and using Amazon to sell them. She's monetizing AdThrive, affiliate sales, and sponsorships, and now she's making around $50,000 a month just on her products on Amazon. Instead of starting out narrow and getting broader, she's actually made her niche more specific and continues to thrive. Her platform is constantly validating new markets for her, from sandals to packing cubes and more, just because of the traffic she built up over time.

Every person I just shared with you started from zero. But they all had their own Take Action Moments, and now they're seeing the take action effect in full force.

NOW IT'S YOUR TURN

When I say there's a market for everything, I really do mean it. Maybe you do have a specific invention that has a unique twist people haven't seen before; it's still going to fall to a market that already exists. I mean, we got our kids into the school we wanted because of landscape bridges. My friend's full-time income happened because of succulents. There's absolutely a market for the thing that you get excited about. The first step to finding the right market isn't to think about the market at all. It's there. The first step is figuring out what it is you actually want to do.

If you haven't identified something (or several things) yet, sit down again with your pad of paper and pen. Go back to that quiet place where you found your why, and let yourself dream a bit. What would you be super excited to work on every single day without getting tired of it? In the same way that I didn't want you to limit your dreams for your perfect day, don't limit your possibilities here. You're not making a permanent life choice. One day in the future, things might change, and you'll start working on something else. That's okay. What would you want to wake up and have to do tomorrow?

Write down your passions and your hobbies. Write down your missions and causes. Write down what it is you do when you're not working. Write down what you *think* about doing while you *are* working. Write down what you're good at. Write down what everyone *else* says you're good at.

If you need to jog your creativity, work through a "touch list" exercise to get started. Start at the beginning of your day and write down every single thing that you touch. (You can also do this with your perfect day—what would you *like* to do every day?) Your quiet, unconscious interests will often pop up on the list, like guitar, piano, crochet, fishing gear, etc.

Don't limit yourself by the income you need or the income you think that thing might bring. Don't limit yourself by your experience or expertise. My podcast started because I'd stumbled on this Amazon thing and decided to share my journey as it unfolded. I educate others as I'm learning myself, and people love that. Yet those same people often hold themselves back because they're not the expert. They don't have a certificate or a diploma in that one thing. Don't let that stop you! People want to relate to someone as they learn and grow, so all you have to do is show up as yourself doing the thing that you love.

VALIDATE YOUR MARKET

Maybe your passion and interests are super clear to you, and you've already got them on hand. Maybe you've got a handful that you're thinking about, or you're still struggling to identify something. We already know that there is a market for it. Let's see if we can niche down your possibilities into the *right* market.

Pick one thing from your list that you love to talk about. Let's use bass fishing again as an example. That's a great interest that definitely has a market! But it's a little too broad. So what aspects of bass fishing do you love? Are you excited about kayak bass fishing? That's more like it. Maybe you're a guitar player, but what *kind* of guitar player? Classical or heavy metal? Jazz? Would you rather play guitar all day long or fish for bass all day? If you want to cook meals all day, would they be easy recipes or gourmet? If you're struggling to answer, it's okay. Stick with me as we keep unfolding this, and you'll get it.

If you're reading this and you already have a business or a market that you want to grow, then use your current market to drill down deeper. Also, you might not be the expert in your business and that's okay. You can always find one and then use this framework to implement these principles for building a future-proof business. Remember, my wife was the photographer and I was the marketer.

Let's stick with bass fishing here and see where it takes us.

When you type "bass fishing" into Google, what comes up? What autofills as things that people are already searching for? What posts come up as the top results? Do the same thing on YouTube now. These quick searches tell you that people are *actually* out there talking about what you want to talk about—probably a lot of people.

When you start to dive deep into that market, you learn so much more. How many people are watching those videos? How many channels are out there talking about your topic? Is the niche you're thinking about represented well? Maybe there's one big channel on bass fishing, but it's more about beginner tips than what you were interested in. You like to talk about tournaments, and that's not represented as well.

If you are still trying to figure out your niche, you can look a little deeper. Google offers free keyword research tools, where all you have to do is type in things like "bass fishing" to see the popular search terms for that topic. Google Trends is another good (free!) tool. It will show you the search traffic for your topic and popular terms that use that phrase. As you read those lists, you'll get a better sense of what you're excited about and how it matches with the content people are publishing and what their readers are looking for.

WHAT IS...*CONTENT PUBLISHING?*

Don't let this phrase turn you off. Even if you're plan-
ning to sell products in an e-commerce store or on
Amazon and nothing else, you're still going to publish
content anyway. Content really is king. It's the best
way to get people's attention, offer them value, and
build the bond that will eventually lead to sales. If you
publish content, people will be able to find it. When
people find it, eventually they'll want to buy something from you. *Publish* just means "post," and *content*
just means talking about your interest in the way that
feels most comfortable to you—writing, speaking, or
on video. That's it! Nothing fancy.

VALIDATE THE MONEY

Last but not least, while you're researching your niche
market, go ahead and validate for yourself that there's
money in it, too. With sales last on the list in our process,
it's easy to get nervous about making money and to want
to jump the gun. We're still going to play the long game
with revenue, but you might want to know here that you
can eventually make money in this market.

One way to validate revenue is to search for your topic on
YouTube. Find a channel that's publishing a lot of content
around that topic and then watch a few of its videos. If ads
are being displayed to you, then you know the owners are
making money. You can't see how much they're making,
of course, but YouTube is definitely a stream of revenue
for them.

Another way is through Amazon. This platform has basically become a search engine for buyers. If your market is in bass fishing, type it into the search bar on Amazon. What kinds of products are being sold to people? Only look at the first page. What products are sponsored? What ads are showing up? You don't have to choose products to sell right now—just know that the products that come up are an idea of what's working in that market.

If you've found blogs on your topic, look around the website. (Note: You can also look on YouTube profiles to find website links. They might have a blog or even a store that they link to from YouTube.) Inside blog posts, look for products that they link to. They're probably collecting affiliate revenue from those links. Look for banner ads. Look for storefronts, subscriptions, and services. Those are all sources of income that they are making within your market.

This should all be exciting information, by the way—not limiting! We're looking at the landscape before we start doing the work. Someone else's talking about your interest doesn't mean they are the only person who can do that thing. Let their work validate the fact that there is *a* market, and then in the next chapter we'll start to develop a strategy to reach *the* market that you're niching down to. Your voice, your perspective, and your angle are all unique.

This book is about taking action for a reason. You've got to choose a market and go for it before you can get any results to work from. Don't be afraid to experiment. Don't be afraid to play. We're doing this on the side for now so that you have the mental and financial space to settle into something you love. When you get that niche right, there's no stopping you.

⚡

TAKE ACTION EXERCISE: NICHING DOWN

First, take some time to research and explore a market. You can start broadly if you need to, but remember we don't stay there. Some discovery will allow you to learn the process, and also see what the potential is in a certain market.

Next, you're going to get more specific with that market. Keep in mind that when we get attention in front of the right people who need us first, we build a solid foundation that can expand later. It's always better to niche down to something narrow when we're just starting out or pivoting an existing business in a new direction. So it's time to niche down!

So think about your interests—that thing that sparks your energy and excitement—explore a market, and then take that interest and make it super specific. What angle do you really want to take? Remember: fishing is broad, bass fishing is better, kayak bass fishing is best.

GET YOUR MARKET'S ATTENTION

Quitting my job was a significant moment in my life, but the direction of my life hadn't really changed until this curious, excited part of me woke up and started to play. The more I learned about marketing, the more I felt at home. I liked to create things—even construction was gratifying because you're building something out of nothing. I liked to help people, and I loved to talk (still do!). Over the years I've discovered that I love helping people, solving problems, and teaching others through the process. But I'm always curious, and that sometimes leads me into less than ideal situations. Remember Amway? You know that story.

Back at my father's construction company, I remember

watching this guy come around every so often to collect money to run print ads for a local coupon book. Imagine about fifty envelope-sized coupons printed onto construction paper and stapled together. That's more or less what these booklets were, all mailed off to different zip codes. Every month, my father and his partner would run a discount coupon (basically an ad) in them.

Wait. Let me get more specific: every month, my father and his partner *paid eight hundred dollars* to be in this coupon booklet. That's $9,600 every year to be in this construction-paper–style set of ads. I started to run the math in my head and thought, *Holy crap, this guy is raking in the cash.*

Fifty businesses at eight hundred each would be $480,000 per year. Even when you factor in printing and postage, that guy was crushing it. So I started to dream up my next *big* idea. I knew of a local printing company that did direct mail pieces for businesses, and a friend of mine did all of the design for them. (In fact, that was Joel—the guy I mentioned earlier who introduced me to Photoshop.) Like me, he was great at his job but similarly frustrated, and somewhere we started to brainstorm. I got pricing from him, he got ideas from me, and we decided to give it a shot—our own coupon booklet.

I still had some cold-calling confidence from the things

I'd read and heard at Amway, and I thought we had it made. All I had to do was knock on some doors and get people who were interested.

You might already be seeing some of the red flags that I missed. This thing had no history. They didn't know me. They had no idea where or that it would actually mail. They had no proof of return. We had no trust at all—and they had no reason to give me any of their time or attention.

But out I went, knocking on doors full of hope.

The first fifteen or twenty businesses were quick nos. I got a couple of maybes, and then one guy who went down as a yes for five hundred bucks. Not great. So I went back out again to another ten businesses. I sent my wife out to some more—maybe a woman's touch would make the difference. Nope.

With only two or three businesses sold, we were going to lose money on printing and shipping. *Okay, so this is harder than it looks.*

I even tried setting up a basic website where we could add extra value by letting them advertise their business there, too. After playing with that idea for a little bit, I realized it was way too much work for the return. With my tail between my legs, I went back to those two or three yeses and gave them their deposits back.

My takeaway from Amway had been reinforced: I did not want to cold-call anymore. I wanted people to come to me, like they did on a job site. I was used to working at people's homes and having a neighbor come over to ask if I could do their bathroom or cabinets or build a new deck.

The people I was going to for Amway and this booklet idea weren't out looking for their own shampoo or a new advertising expense. I had to chase them down and convince them, and it hadn't worked out well for me. Instead, I wanted people to be on the lookout for something and find me. Let them sell themselves on my services as they got to know what I had to offer. I wanted to earn their attention rather than demanding it.

Photography work runs in cycles, and there's definitely an off-season where things get slow. I had to figure out how to bring more people in, which means I had to draw on what I'd learned about marketing and start to experiment even more.

Without learning about marketing through all the ups and downs over the years, I would never be where I am today. More importantly, I wouldn't have found out that I really enjoy it. The successful businesses I've built since then all came from what I've learned about getting attention and attracting the right customers. Sometimes you have to wade through things that don't work, and that's okay. As long as you keep learning as you take action, you'll find that thing you love that meets your market's need.

TIMING IS EVERYTHING

No one is expecting to buy an expensive vacuum cleaner when the Kirby guy comes around. When you solicit people for a sale when they aren't ready for you—not even in the market for what you have—you have to work to get any traction. You have to ask to meet the manager or convince them to let you in the door. You have to do a ton of educating and a lot of legwork, and you have to be really okay with rejections.

With all of the tools that we have available to us in this moment in time, why would we work so hard at sales?

The conversion is so much easier when you can get people to raise their hands first. Once they come to you with interest, you've got their attention without even working for it. When you hold their attention with great content and value, you can start to build a relationship. Then, when the time is right to offer a product or service, the sale seems easy. All of the legwork happened along the way instead of you trying to do it all up front on a cold call.

If I were making a coupon mailer now (to be clear, I probably wouldn't do that), I would have paid $1,000 to send a mailer out to the businesses first. Then they could see the quality and know that I actually do send mail. They'd see that I invested in them first, and then I'd leave my contact info on the mailer. If they wanted more information, they could call me.

(Side note: Today, I would probably also have used my father's business numbers—his rate of return—to help demonstrate it works. I know the mailers worked for him. Every time one would get sent, we would have tons of calls and jobs would be sold. Plus, now that I've been learning direct response marketing over the past fifteen years, I could create better sales copy to help get people excited and interested. By taking action over and over again, I have a huge range of experiences to draw from when I want to start something new.)

The difference in this type of marketing versus going door to door is they would be calling me. It'd be much more efficient than knocking on doors and seeing who says yes. That kind of approach leaves people feeling ambushed— or at least annoyed. I like to think of this as magnetic marketing, where we attract the right people with a message and then when they show interest, we tell them what we have that can help them. It's way easier this way.

WHAT IS...*AMBUSH MARKETING*?

The old-fashioned marketing method I used at Amway— knocking on doors and pitching to cousins at the dinner table—has gotten worse in the digital age. Now, instead of going to see ten of your friends in person, you make calls, text, email, post on Facebook, start a group, send direct messages...pretty soon, you've hassled all of your friends so much that they cringe when you show up. Instead of shifting to some healthier strategies, people have started ambush marketing. They'll start a thirty-day challenge, but before the first day is over they're already trying to sell you something. The pitch comes before the prospective client experiences any value from what they're being offered. Take your time. Don't sell anything until you've offered plenty of value to someone who is interested and has built a bond with you and your business.

Even with the right tools, a bid for attention that shows up at the wrong time can be a turnoff. Let's say I run a Facebook ad that's going to you, even though you don't care about learning how to sell online, on Amazon, or how to create a business. You're scrolling through your sister's bridal shower pictures, enjoying the moment, and then BAM—a big message from me that says, "Let me show you how to launch products on Amazon!"

Is that really the right timing?

People go to Facebook to get away from *stuff*. They're taking a break from work. They're unwinding. They might even be in a bad mood because they saw that Suzie said something they didn't like. Without careful targeting (which can be done, of course), it's easy to get in front of people at the wrong time.

The other mishap in that example would be trying to sell too early, too. The timing of your offer is everything, which is why we put sales at the very end of this framework. I'm much more likely to make an ad that says, "Hey, I thought you'd like to know that these three things can help with your Amazon business: A, B, and C. Hope you enjoyed this! Share it with someone who might think it's valuable. Talk to you later." Then, because it doesn't ask anything of them at all, I can be a little bit more comfortable with my ad placement and timing as long as my targeting is right for my niche.

If they're interested in more of what I have to offer, they will come back to me. They can choose to take action or not, but either way I've given them something of value.

When I create content, I know that 95 percent of my audience may never buy a thing right away. But 5 percent of them will pay me very well. I know it's hard not to think about sales when you're not making money yet, but it'll come. For now, focus on getting in front of everyone inside your market. You can make an offer of help when the timing is right.

BE HELPFUL, BE YOURSELF

Now that we know we don't have to cold-call, and we know not to blast a sales pitch all over the place, let's look at our options for getting attention. To do this, we need to think about our market again. If you've been working through these steps as we talked about them, you should have already found a good, broad market. Then you niched it down and validated that there are people interested in it and buying things (or clicking links). So we know there are people out there, ready to pay attention to someone. Now we need to figure out what they're looking for and where they are showing up to look for it.

Are they looking for video tutorials on YouTube or podcast discussions on iTunes? Are they going straight to Google for articles or asking their friends on Twitter? Are they skimming images on Pinterest or searching hashtags on Instagram? If you're reading this book ten years from now, the platforms will no doubt have changed, but the principle stays the same. Where are your people hanging out, and how do they want to consume information? Identify where they are, and meet them there with what they're looking for that is helpful.

Possibly the most important part of this is meeting them with helpful content. To be helpful, we've already talked about not giving them a sales pitch. We also can't show up as someone else. It's hard to build a bond with someone who isn't being authentic. You have to ask yourself what you're comfortable doing. Obviously, all new things feel a little uncomfortable. That's not what I mean. I mean don't start with a podcast just because I have one if you're a born writer and your market loves to read. Remember, you're coming into this market with your perspective and personality. You've got to be true to who you are to make that work!

Remember, you don't have to be an expert to be helpful. People used to come up to us during a photography shoot or if they saw that we were carrying a camera and ask what kind of equipment we were using. We'd gone from "how are you possibly going to do photography" to photography being the thing everyone asks us about. It was almost appealing that we weren't experts who knew everything there was to know. That made us trustworthy and reliable—we had been where they were, and we had shortcuts that could help them do well much faster than we had.

There are three categories of content that we can create: audio, video, and text. My strengths are audio and video, which is why this book was such a long time coming. I stayed with my strengths until I was ready to stretch myself. Just because you're not good at one of those things doesn't mean you can't get there. For now, start with what comes naturally to you. If you're starting a new venture or adding something to an existing business, you want to focus on the content and process—not your paralyzing camera fright or banging your head against the keyboard.

Now, let's quickly validate again. If your market is on YouTube and you know you want to make videos, go back and do your keyword exercise again there. Type in your topic and see what comes up. Again, we're still not mapping out the "how" of any of this content. That will come next, in chapter 8. Right now, we just need an idea of what kinds of things will get the attention of your market and how you'll feel most confident when you meet them there. Let YouTube autofill so it brings up suggestions for you. Can you quickly spot five video topics? Are those things that you could talk about? Of course they are. This is your *big thing*. You've got this.

NO GAMES, NO GIMMICKS

You might have noticed I haven't given you any search

engine optimization (SEO) tricks. That's because there aren't any. Back in the day, probably five years ago, you could niche down to a topic—say, losing belly fat—then buy a domain like howtolosebellyfat.com Because that topic was in the title of your web address, Google's crawlers would index you for that search term. *They must really know how to lose belly fat. It says so right here!*

There were other aspects that Google rewarded sites for, too, like how many links went to a page and how many times keywords showed up in articles. Those things are still factors, but not as much. People figured out how to game the system. They'd get a whole bunch of links to point to the website or have useless articles filled with keywords, and for a little while, Google rewarded that.

And then the Google Slap happened. They got tired of people being artificially ranked higher and changed all of their requirements. Overnight, pages that had been showing up as top results got dropped completely out of search results, nowhere to be found.

There are probably still ways to game the system, but I honestly stopped trying to keep up. What I do know for sure is that there are plenty of people succeeding without any games at all. They've built legit sites and channels that people want to come back to. They've got legit links pointing to them because of their high-value content.